iPod® and iTunes®
QuickSteps

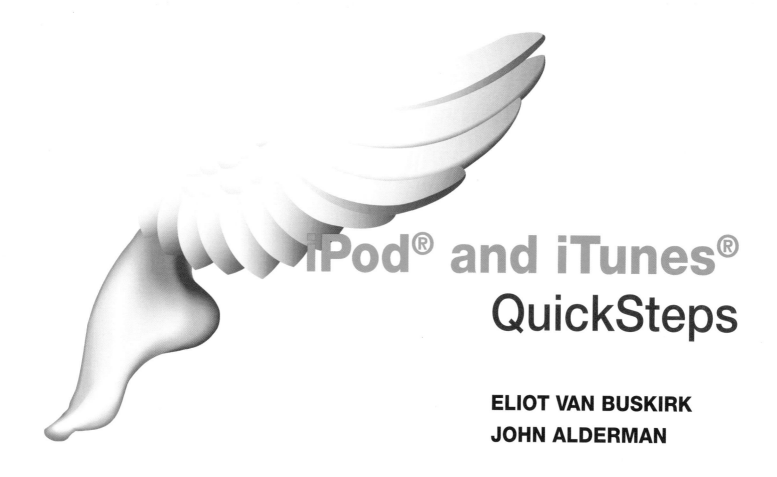

iPod® and iTunes®
QuickSteps

ELIOT VAN BUSKIRK

JOHN ALDERMAN

McGraw-Hill/Osborne

New York   Chicago   San Francisco
Lisbon   London   Madrid   Mexico City
Milan   New Delhi   San Juan
Seoul   Singapore   Sydney   Toronto

McGraw-Hill/Osborne

2100 Powell Street, 10th Floor
Emeryville, California 94608
U.S.A.

To arrange bulk purchase discounts for sales promotions, premiums, or fund-raisers, please contact **McGraw-Hill**/Osborne at the above address.

This book was composed with Adobe® InDesign®.

Information has been obtained by **McGraw-Hill**/Osborne from sources believed to be reliable. However, because of the possibility of human or mechanical error by our sources, **McGraw-Hill**/Osborne, or others, **McGraw-Hill**/Osborne does not guarantee the accuracy, adequacy, or completeness of any information and is not responsible for any errors or omissions or the results obtained from the use of such information.

iPOD® AND iTUNES® QUICKSTEPS

1234567890 WCK WCK 0198765

ISBN 0-07-226253-2

ACQUISITIONS EDITOR / Marjorie McAneny

PROJECT EDITOR / LeeAnn Pickrell

ACQUISITIONS COORDINATOR / Agatha Kim

COPY EDITOR / Sally Engelfried

PROOFREADER / Paul Tyler

INDEXER / Valerie Perry

COMPOSITION / G & S Book Services

ILLUSTRATION / G & S Book Services

SERIES DESIGN / Bailey Cunningham

COVER DESIGN / Pattie Lee

To all those who have been unnecessarily perplexed by confusing technology.

About the Authors

Eliot Van Buskirk is the Technology Editor of MP3.com, a division of CNET Networks. Van Buskirk's *MP3 Insider* column is the longest-running single-writer column at CNET.com, the largest online tech publication in the world. Winner of the Maggie Award for Best Online Column of 2003, *MP3 Insider* is regularly featured on MP3.com, CNET.com, ZDNET.com, and News.com. Van Buskirk is frequently featured in the mainstream and bloggish media as an authority on digital music (CNN, Boing Boing, NPR, the BBC, PBS, "CBS Evening News," Phil Leigh's Media Blog, *San Francisco Chronicle*, KFOG, *Smart Money Magazine*, *USA Today*, *Time Magazine Online*, and more.

John Alderman is a digital music expert, musician, and author. Since 1995, he has been covering online music in editorial positions with such leading technology publications as CNET, Wired News, and HotWired.com. He has also written for *The Guardian, Salon.com, Details, Mondo 2000,* and *Yahoo Internet Life*, and has spoken on the topic of digital media at conferences and in appearances on CNN, BBC, NPR, and others. His widely acclaimed book, *Sonic Boom: Napster, MP3, and the New Pioneers of Music,* was a New York Times Notable Book of the Year for 2002.

Contents at a Glance

Contents

Chapter 3 **Using Your iPod** 33

Chapter 4 **Taking Control of iTunes** 47

Chapter 7 Supercharging Your iPod 101

Chapter 8 Playing Music at Home 117

Chapter 9 Tapping into Advanced Audio Sources 135

Chapter 10 Becoming an iPod Jedi (the Next Level) 155

A Appendix

Acknowledgments

Thanks to everyone who has contributed to making the digital music revolution nearly as revolutionary as I had hoped it would be and to those who will take us the rest of the way. Thanks also to Ria, CNET cohorts past and present, "Lymie" the Deer Tick, and the McGraw-Hill/Osborne team (Margie McAneny, Agatha Kim, LeeAnn Pickrell).

Thanks to John Alderman for pulling extra weight while I dealt with a bug.

Honorary Mentions: Friday Foosball League, all the folks at MP3.com, my musical family, Show "Mr. Show" Lah, Fraunhofer Gesellschaft, Eiger Labs, Shawn Fanning, Sen. Rick Boucher, EFF.org, Steve Jobs, Halsey Minor, Lawrence Lessig, Synaptic, Danika Cleary, Kevin Wood, my lucky stars.
—*Eliot Van Buskirk*

Thanks to all who have fought hard, thought deeply, and looked into their souls to bring art to the world. It may be easier than ever to hear their creations, but their work often remains fraught with danger and hardship.

Thanks to Eliot, for inviting me to collaborate on this book; to the same trio he thanked at McGraw-Hill/Osborne (Margie McAneny, Agatha Kim, LeeAnn Pickrell); and to Peter McGuigan for his ever-helpful advice. Thanks to Three Day Stubble for years of fun.

Finally, a special thanks to my mother for giving me a love of music, my sister for sharing her records, and to my wife for helping me to live my dreams.
—*John Alderman*

Introduction

QuickSteps books are recipe books for computer users. They answer the question "How do I...?" by providing a quick set of steps to accomplish the most common tasks with a particular program or device. The sets of steps are the central focus of the book. QuickSteps sidebars provide information on how to do many small functions or tasks that are in support of the primary functions quickly. QuickFacts sidebars supply information that you need to know about a subject. Notes, Tips, and Cautions augment the steps, but they are presented in a separate column so as not to interrupt the flow. Brief introductions are present, but there is minimal narrative otherwise. Many illustrations and figures are also included where they support the steps.

QuickSteps books are organized by function and the tasks needed to perform that function. Each function is a chapter. Each task, or "How To," contains the steps needed for accomplishing the function with the relevant Notes, Tips, Cautions, and screenshots. Tasks are easy to find through:

- The Table of Contents, which lists the functional areas (chapters) and tasks in the order they are presented
- A How-To list of tasks on the opening page of each chapter
- The index, which provides an alphabetical list of the terms that are used to describe the functions and tasks
- Color-coded tabs for each chapter or functional area with an index to the tabs in the Contents at a Glance (just before the Table of Contents)

Conventions Used in this Book

iPod and iTunes QuickSteps uses several conventions designed to make the book easier for you to follow. Conventions used include:

- A in the Table of Contents and in the How-To list in each chapter references a QuickSteps sidebar and a references a QuickFacts sidebar.

- **Bold** type is used for words or objects on the screen that you are to do something with, like click **Save As**, open **File**, and click **Close**.

- *Italic type* is used for a word or phrase that is being defined or otherwise deserves special emphasis.

- Underlined type is used for text that you are to type from the keyboard.

- SMALL CAPITAL LETTERS are used for keys on the keyboard such as ENTER and SHIFT.

- When you are expected to enter a command, you are told to press the key(s). If you are to enter text or numbers, you are told to type them.

How To...

Chapter 1
Getting to Know Your iPod

This chapter introduces you to your new companion, the iPod. We'll take a quick look at the history of the iPod, note the types available, open the box, and set up your computer to play along nicely. We'll also explain some important principles about how the iPod works, and offer a few tips so that you'll be able to get long life and best use from whichever model you've chosen.

Understand Apple's iPod Line: A Quick Rundown

The Apple iPod was by no means the first MP3 player—that distinction belongs to the Saehan/Eiger Labs F10. Hardly as catchy as "the iPod," is it? Apple's little white wonder burst onto the scene about two years later in November of 1999— the first to use a smaller, 1.8″ hard drive to store 5GB of music, with a scroll wheel for breezing through thousands of songs in seconds. Since then, the iPod

NOTE

The number of songs you can fit onto an iPod depends on how much memory, or capacity, it has. This is denoted in megabytes (MB) or gigabytes (GB). You can fit about 20 CDs' worth of music onto 1 GB of memory. We say "about," because the number of songs you can fit depends a lot on how much the files are compressed, a.k.a. their bit rate (if you don't know what that all means, don't worry—you will soon enough).

TIP

Start charging now! We'll cover installation later, but before you can use your iPod, it'll need to be 100 percent charged. Connect whichever included cable fits the jack in the square white power adapter, fold out its retractable plugs, and plug it into a power outlet. Connect the other end of the cable to the iPod—you'll feel it snap in and see the Apple logo on the iPod's screen (unless you have a screenless Shuffle model—more on those soon), and the charging will commence. Again, let the power adapter run its course until your iPod is completely charged—four hours should do it for all models. This is probably the most nail-biting part of the iPod experience: waiting to actually use your hot new machine.

line has expanded dramatically, giving you new ways of storing and accessing your music. Here's a rundown on the whole line in chronological order, from the ones you'll find on store shelves to older iPods you can pick up on eBay.

First-Generation iPod (a.k.a. "1G")

This original iPod (Figure 1-1) has a mechanical scroll wheel control that physically rotates, with four buttons around it for **Menu**, **Play**, **Fast Forward**, and **Rewind**. At the center of the scroll wheel is a round button for **Select**, which is the only control that's remained more or less unaltered through most of the subsequent iPod line. The initial hard drive capacity was 5GB, but Apple released a 10GB unit too. Both connect to your computer with a standard Firewire cable.

Capacities　　5GB and 10GB
Connection　　Firewire

Second-Generation iPod (2G)

This one (Figure 1-2) is identical to the first-generation iPod, except its scroll wheel is touch-sensitive (Apple calls it a touch wheel). The Firewire port's on the top of the player, as with the iPod 1G.

Capacities　　10GB and 20GB
Connection　　Firewire

Figure 1-1: A first-generation iPod's battery is likely shot by now, but they, like other aging iPods, can be rehabilitated (see Chapter 10).

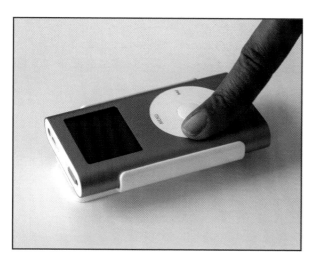

Figure 1-2: *Slide your finger around the touch-sensitive scroll wheel to cruise through songs and menus.*

NOTE

Due to the MP3 format's early prevalence in digital music, iPods and similar devices are usually called "MP3 players" as shorthand, even when they also play other digital music file types. We've included a full list of what your iPod can play, along with explanations of each file type, in Chapter 2.

NOTE

Apple says that the included armband adds enough shock resistance for jogging, but we still recommend the Shuffle (discussed soon) for hardcore joggers.

Third-Generation iPod (3G)

Apple replaced the buttons around the scroll wheel of the 3G iPod (Figure 1-3) with four round orange-backlit buttons located between the scroll wheel and the screen. They sure look cool in the dark, but some users complained that the touch-sensitive buttons were a bit fussy. One big advantage is the dock, which holds the player safely at an attractive angle and includes connections for your stereo and computer.

Capacities   10GB, 15GB, 20GB, 30GB, and 40GB

Connections   Firewire and USB

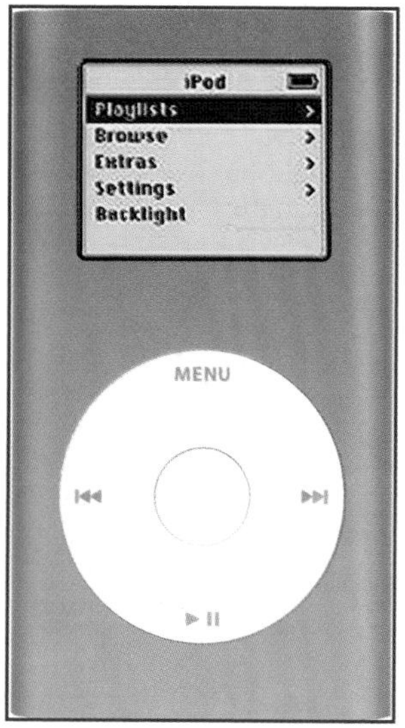

Figure 1-4: *The iPod Mini's metal chassis makes it pretty rugged, as well as just plain pretty.*

iPod Mini

The first iPod to be available in five colors, the iPod Mini (Figure 1-4) was initially a big departure from the iPod line because it housed a smaller, lower-capacity 1-inch hard drive. The other new addition—another in Apple's long history of design breakthroughs—was the clickable scroll wheel, which replaced the four touch-sensitive buttons found on the 3G iPod. You click each of the four quarters of the click wheel for **Play**, **Rewind**, **Fast Forward**, and **Menu**.

Capacity   4GB

Connections   Firewire and USB

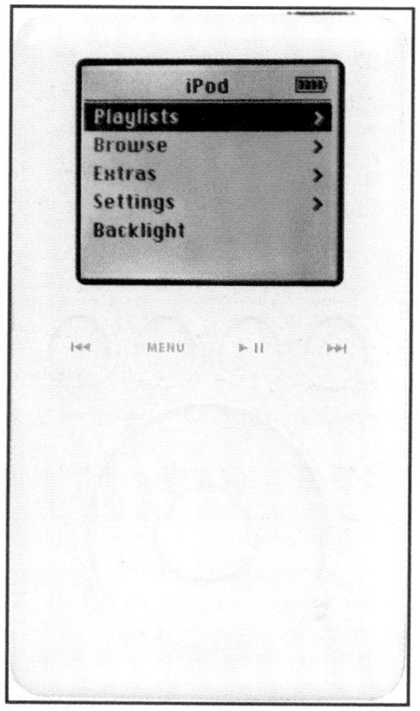

Figure 1-3: *Apple refined its design to allow for a thinner, more rounded profile in the third-generation iPod that has lasted into subsequent generations.*

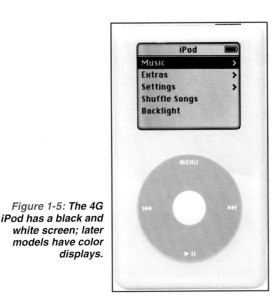

Figure 1-5: The 4G iPod has a black and white screen; later models have color displays.

NOTE

Rapper 50 Cent uses a U2 iPod, which he said was given to him by Bono of U2.

Fourth-Generation iPod (4G)

The 4G iPod (Figure 1-5) melds the sleek profile of the 3G iPod with the much-improved click wheel of the iPod Mini. As with many previous models, the larger capacity option is ever-so-slightly thicker to accommodate the larger hard drive.

Capacities   20GB and 40GB

Connections   Firewire and USB

THE HP iPOD

Although it has since been discontinued, HP used to sell its own specially branded 4G iPod, which was identical to the one that Apple sells except for the fact that Hewlett-Packard supplies support rather than Apple (not that you would need it, with this book in hand). Like other earlier iPods, the HP models are available only in the secondhand market.

THE U2 iPOD

Another acronym—U2—designates a rarer 4G iPod variant: the Apple iPod U2 Special Edition, which sports a red click wheel set strikingly against a shiny black shell. It kicked off an extensive iPod ad campaign involving (who else?) the band U2 and features engraved signatures of the band on the back. Along with it, Apple offers a $50 discount on buying the complete U2 catalog from the iTunes Music Store (we'll get to the store soon).

iPod Photo

The iPod Photo (Figure 1-6) was the first iPod with a color screen. As its color screen migrated to other models in the iPod line, the name "iPod Photo" was discontinued since those photo features became available on other models with color screens. It's great for scrolling through your digital photos, but that's not all: the color factor also gives you album art for your music and a more vibrant navigation experience. Since Summer 2005, all standard iPods (not Mini or Shuffle) come with color screens and all the functions of the iPod Photo.

Capacities   40GB and 60GB

Connections   Firewire and USB

Figure 1-6: *The first iPod with a color screen, the iPod Photo added the ability to display photos.*

iPod Shuffle

The baby of the family, this one uses flash memory, which means no moving parts to be jostled (and potentially break) and much less battery drain. Its small size allows the Shuffle (Figure 1-7) to be perfectly pocketable. This thin, screenless iPod plugs right into an empty USB port on your computer (or even a USB hub in, say, your flat panel monitor), from which it draws power and music without the need for cables.

Capacities	512MB and 1GB
Connection	Direct USB plug-in

Figure 1-7: *The iPod Shuffle is ideal for grabbing a few hours of tunes for a quick jaunt or jog.*

iPod Mini 2G

Never one to leave well enough alone, Apple updated the iPod Mini with minor alterations (there's no gold color option, the icons on the click wheel match the color of the chassis, battery life is vastly improved, and the power adapter is optional).

Capacities	4GB and 6GB
Connections	Firewire and USB

The Standard Late-Generation White iPod

When Apple added a color screen to all white dockable iPods, it essentially turned them into iPod Photos, obviating the need for a distinction between the two models. The new color white-dockable iPods launched in 20GB and 60GB capacities (the 60GB model is slightly thicker and heavier, due to having a dual-platter hard drive).

Capacities	20GB and 60GB
Connections	Firewire and USB

NOTE

If you live with other people and they don't already have MP3 players, there's a good chance they're going to want one too. Luckily, you can use multiple iPods on the same computer, so family members or roommates can get in on the fun, even if there's just one computer in the house.

QUICKFACTS

POTENTIAL iPODS OF THE FUTURE

We expect many more iPods from Apple since the folks who make iPod parts are always coming up with ways to pack more music power and features into ever-shrinking packages. Be that as it may, Apple tends not to alter too much in terms of operation, so just about everything in this book will apply to future models. Stuff we might expect to see from iPod and iTunes future iterations:

- Higher capacities at smaller sizes (a given for any tech gadget)
- New colors (maybe even black? Darth iPod?)
- Audio/voice recording
- Video playback
- Wireless connections (Bluetooth, Wifi, wireless USB connections to headphones, computers, cell phones, satellite, car stereo, and/or other MP3 players)
- Home models (you can hook your iPod up to a stereo or use Airport Express for music in the home, both of which we'll get to later, but there's still no iPod Home unit)
- iTunes on certain cell phones (we're looking at you, Motorola)

CAUTION

Technology never stops trundling forward, which can cause despondency when your new toy is no longer the latest model. This isn't the way to think! Later models will always offer new bells and whistles; it's just the nature of the beast. The fact of the matter is that if something still does what you bought it for, it's a good purchase no matter what comes out later. You should only upgrade if a new product's going to give you something your old one can't (as can admittedly be the case sometimes).

iPod Nano

In the worthy interest of making technology ever smaller, Apple released the Nano in the Fall of 2005. Unlike all other iPods, aside from the Shuffle, the Nano uses flash memory (its advantages: small size, no skipping, low power consumption). Unlike the Shuffle, the Nano has a screen, so you can navigate as you would with any other iPod with a screen. Other than the special edition U2 iPod, the Nano is the first iPod Apple has sold in the color black. Of course, it also comes in white (Figure 1-8). Those wishing to add more color can do so using carrying cases sold by Apple.

*Figure 1-8: **The iPod Nano is available in black or white.***

| **Capacities** | 2GB and 4GB |
| **Connections** | USB |

Choose the Right iPod(s)

Now that there are so many iPod models out there, it's no longer enough, as it was back in '99, to say, "Just gimme an iPod." We ran down the models; the best way to choose which one's right for you is to ask yourself a few key questions. Who knows, you might even end up with two, since they each have their advantages.

How Will You Use It?

If you want to use your iPod to view photos, an iPod with a color screen is a must. On the other hand, joggers, electronics droppers, and bargain hunters should consider the iPod Shuffle, since it's the smallest, cheapest, and most resilient of the iPod line. For many people, a 20GB iPod seems to hit the sweet spot because it holds an entire music collection, usually with room to spare. But for those who need a smaller device and don't mind refreshing the music

TIP

People like to upgrade their iPods to the latest model. If you don't mind carrying around last year's model (and potentially following our advice on battery replacement in Chapter 10), consider turning their upgrade into your great deal.

TIP

It's increasingly common for digital audio fanatics to own two players: one hard-drive based for regular commuting and longer trips, and one solid state flash for moments of bouncing and sweat. If you can afford to own two, we certainly recommend it.

QUICKSTEPS

UNDERSTANDING THE BIG PICTURE

With all the ads for the iPod and other MP3 players we encounter these days, you'd think everyone would understand how these things work. But the switch from CD players to the iPod is much bigger than any format leap people have ever been asked to contend with. Here's how the new digital deal works, in case this is your first MP3 player.

1. Get music files onto your computer.
2. Transfer tunes onto your iPod.
3. Keep your iPod's music and software updated.
4. Protect, tune up, and accessorize as needed.

on their iPods every once in a while, an iPod Nano fits the bill. Thinking about which category you fit into will help you make the right choice; you may even find that you need a second iPod (for example, you might want a 20GB iPod for the car and a 512MB iPod Shuffle for jogging).

What's Your Budget?

The main factor in determining how much an iPod costs is its capacity (i.e., how much music it can hold). Once you've figured out which model you want, there's still the matter of memory to consider since most iPods come in various capacities. If you already have MP3s or other digital music files on your computer, consider importing them into iTunes (for directions, see Chapter 2). The bottom of the iTunes window can tell you how big your collection is in gigabytes (GB). If most of your music is coming from CD, calculate how much room you'll need (20 standard CDs take up about 1GB). No need to get too nitpicky—just keep in mind that you should only pay for the capacity you need.

What Connections Does Your Computer Have?

If you have a new computer and a new iPod, they'll get along swimmingly in terms of connections—either way, the box includes a cable you can use. However, if you bargain hunt for an older model of iPod or you have an older computer, make sure your computer has the connection required by the iPod you're thinking about getting (Firewire, Figure 1-9; USB, Figure 1-10).

***Figure 1-9:* A computer's Firewire port**

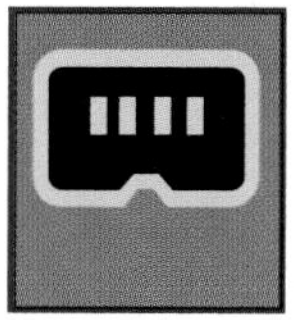

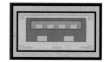

***Figure 1-10:* A computer's USB port**

Prep Your iPod for Play

Now you're ready to roll up your sleeves and get started with the installation process.

TIP

If you bought your iPod from someone else and it didn't come with a CD, or you lost your own copy, you can download the latest version of iTunes directly from Apple. Just point your web browser to http://www.apple.com/itunes/download/. From there you can choose your operating system and download iTunes for free.

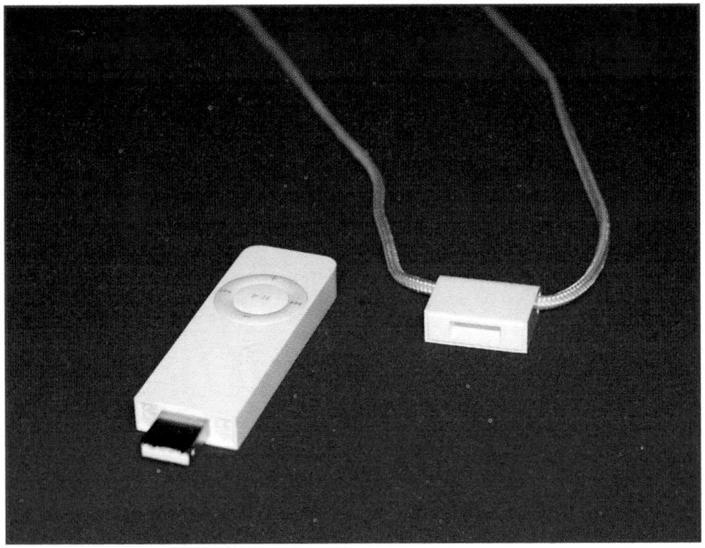

Open the Box

The iPod Shuffle's box is pretty minimal, as fits its less-is-more style. Other models have an origami-like puzzle box complete with a compelling call to audio hedonism: "Designed by Apple in California. Enjoy." It's slick, but now's the time to rip it open! Everything should be nestled in its place, awaiting your discovery.

Take a quick look. Be sure to check that you have everything listed here— especially if you bought your iPod secondhand.

Figure 1-11: *The iPod Shuffle's lanyard attaches via the USB cap.*

CONTENTS OF THE BOXES, BY MODEL

- **iPod Shuffle**   iPod Shuffle; USB cap (this comes attached); Apple earphones; lanyard (basically a rope necklace with another USB cap attached, Figure 1-11); guidebook; a notecard with directions; iPod CD

- **iPod Mini**   iPod Mini; belt clip; iPod dock connector to Firewire cable; iPod dock connector to USB 2 cable; iPod power adapter; Apple earphones; guidebook; iPod CD

- **iPod (white, dockable)**   iPod; iPod dock (with some earlier models); iPod dock connector to Firewire cable; iPod dock connector to USB 2 cable; iPod power adapter; Apple earphones; guidebook; iPod CD

- **iPod Photo**   iPod Photo; belt clip; iPod dock; iPod dock connector to Firewire cable; iPod dock connector to USB 2 cable; iPod power adapter; Apple earphones; guidebook; iPod CD

- **iPod Nano**   iPod Nano; white earbud headphones (regardless of Nano color); USB cable; dock adapter (for connecting to the iPod dock, available separately)

TIP

The puny-looking headphones bundled with your iPod are actually pretty good. But if you're still unsatisfied due to an uncomfortable fit or the merely adequate sound quality, don't despair! In Chapters 5 and 7 we'll discuss accessories for your iPod, including other headphones.

In addition the boxes contain various packaging, some Apple stickers, and printed warranties.

Install iTunes

Now's the time to get your computer and iPod working in sync. You'll need to install the iTunes software, which works like an iPod command center (as well as a pretty great music player in its own right).

CAUTION

If you're thinking of using a case to protect your iPod from scratches, start right away. On the other hand, the iPod was designed to be used without a case, and many people would rather show off Apple's design for reasons of style and convenience. If you're interested in a case, see our section on iPod accessories in Chapter 7.

QUICKSTEPS

CONNECTING YOUR iPOD

Now your computer and iPod begin to communicate with one another.

1. **Configure iPod**   You'll be asked to plug in your iPod. Connect the cable to your computer's USB port; or, if you have a dock, set the iPod in that and connect the dock to your USB port. Then click **OK**.

2. **Serial Number**   Find your registration number, printed in a font size so small it could be used in an eye exam, on the back of your iPod.

3. **License Agreement**   Don't you love these contracts? If you agree to the terms (and we're sure you've read them all!) click **Yes** and proceed.

Continued . . .

START THE INSTALLATION

The first part of installation is all about identity. iTunes wants to know who you are and what language you speak.

1. Slide the iPod CD into your computer and wait a moment—it should start automatically.

2. Choose a language: since you're reading this book, we assume it's English.

3. Choose a country: where do you live?

4. Enter your serial number: you can find it on the back of your iPod (see the QuickSteps sidebar), printed in very tiny type. (Since Apple's design is usually so good, we have to wonder: Is the size of this print designed to be a deterrent for older users, to keep the iPod cool?)

5. Enter your registration data (Figure 1-12): Just the facts.

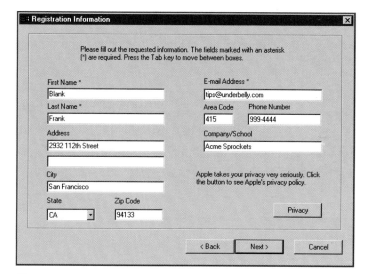

Figure 1-12: **Fill out your registration information.**

CONNECTING YOUR iPOD

(Continued)

4. **Information** A dialog box appears with the latest information about the iTunes software. Read or skim it, and click **Next**.

5. **iTunes Setup Type** Do you want a desktop shortcut for iTunes to make startup easy? If so, check that box. Do you want iTunes to be your default audio player, or do you have another favorite? (Don't sweat any of these decisions too much. iTunes will still work with any option, and it's easy enough to switch your settings after installation.) Click **Next**.

6. **Choose Destination Location** Unless you have a very custom filing system, you'll probably want to stick with the default location for iTunes to be installed. So just click **Next**.

7. **Restart Computer** Check **Yes**, then click **Finish** to restart your computer.

8. **Once your computer is back up, the iPod Assistant dialog comes up on your screen** to finish off some parts of the installation.

TIP

Battery life is a fundamental issue with iPods. It's possible to get the rechargeable battery in your iPod replaced, but it's not easy. Smart users can extend their iPod battery's life by only charging it when its power is depleted. We'll talk more about dealing with the battery in Chapter 3.

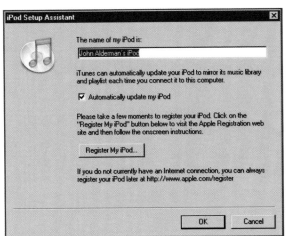

Figure 1-13: ***Use the iPod Setup Assistant to name your iPod, set your syncing preference, and register with Apple.***

iPOD ASSISTANT

The iPod Setup Assistant dialog (Figure 1-13) will now guide you through some key points.

1. Name your iPod: Make up something clever or just call it by your name (the default).

2. Decide whether you want iPod to automatically mirror your music library. This probably depends on the size of your iPod and the size of your music library. If your library is larger, you should not automatically update—there's just not enough space. You'll need to decide just what you want on your iPod and load it manually. (We'll show you how to do that in Chapter 3.)

3. Click **Register My iPod** to visit Apple's registration site. We recommend this because it's always good to have a record of your iPod, in case something goes wrong.

4. Now the fun begins: you'll learn to load up your iPod with music in Chapter 2.

How To...

Chapter 2
Importing Music to iTunes and iPod

We don't profess to have heard the sound of one hand clapping, but it's surely a lot like that of an iPod with no songs. Unlike a CD player, tape deck, record player, or Minidisc player, the iPod doesn't accept removable media. Instead of loading physical music directly onto the iPod, you first load it into iTunes from all kinds of sources. Once it's organized in iTunes, you can transfer music from your computer's hard drive to the iPod's hard drive. We'll get to some more advanced audio sources in Chapter 9; for now, let's cover some iTunes basics and then get some music onto your iPod.

Welcome to iTunes

Apple's iTunes software gives you an abundance of ways to deal with your music, especially compared to your typical CD player. As far as music software goes, critics generally favor its design and ease of use. Let's take a tour of the iTunes interface—your new digital music dashboard.

The Main iTunes Interface

Here's a basic roadmap to familiarize you with the layout (Figure 2-1).

Figure 2-1: *The default iTunes setup is laid out fairly clearly. Click any item in the left pane to bring up its view in the main pane.*

SEARCHING AND BROWSING

To the upper right of the iTunes window, you'll see a **Search** box and an **eye symbol** with the word "Browse" under it (Figure 2-2). They're powerful search assistants, just waiting to help you find tracks in your library. Although you have yet to import music into the iTunes Library, here's a quick introduction to Search and Browse:

- **Search**   This box lets you search for any song or group of songs in your library. If you only enter a few characters, it'll surface any songs that have those characters in them, before you even press ENTER. Cool.

- **Browse**   Click this and you get the **Genre**, **Artist**, and **Album** panes depicted in Figure 2-2. You can click any of those words to sort the respective lists, scroll through them, and click anything in those panes to see the songs that correspond to that attribute. For instance, in Figure 2-2, we clicked the band 101 Strings/Yma Sumac to display their songs in the list below.

iTUNES WINDOW PANES EXPLAINED

Apple designed iTunes to give you the easiest access to stuff you'll end up using iTunes for the most: importing CDs, listening to music, buying songs, organizing your digital music library, and transferring songs to your iPod. But you can adapt its look quite easily. For instance, start typing in the **Search** box. The contents of the library changes to show only songs that have some information that matches the letters you've typed. You'll also see a number of new buttons along the top to help you further sort those results (Figure 2-2).

Figure 2-2: Once you start typing in the Search box, buttons pop up to help you sort the matching results by a number of categories (All, Music, Audiobooks, Podcasts, Videos, and Booklets).

Source

The **Source** pane, located at the upper left of iTunes (Figure 2-3), looks deceptively simple, but it holds the key to several types of music content: **Party Shuffle** (an instant playlist), iTunes **Radio** (free Internet music stations), audio CDs, the iTunes **Music Store**, a few premade Smart Playlists (more on those in Chapter 4), and playlists you've created yourself.

Album Art

Depending on where you obtained a specific song, this pane may or may not display album art (Figure 2-4). Songs purchased from the iTunes Music Store always have album art; songs from CDs you import into iTunes often have art; digital music files obtained from other sources often have no art included.

Song List

When you click anything in the **Source** pane or in any of the three small **Browse** panes, the song list—the main pane that takes up most of the screen—displays all of the songs that correspond to whatever you picked

Figure 2-3: The Source pane helps you access your music in all sorts of ways.

Figure 2-4: By dragging the divider line between the album art and song list panes, you can make the album art display at a larger size, which gives you a better view.

> **TIP**
>
> To add album art to any song, just drag an image into the **album art** pane at the lower left as the song plays.

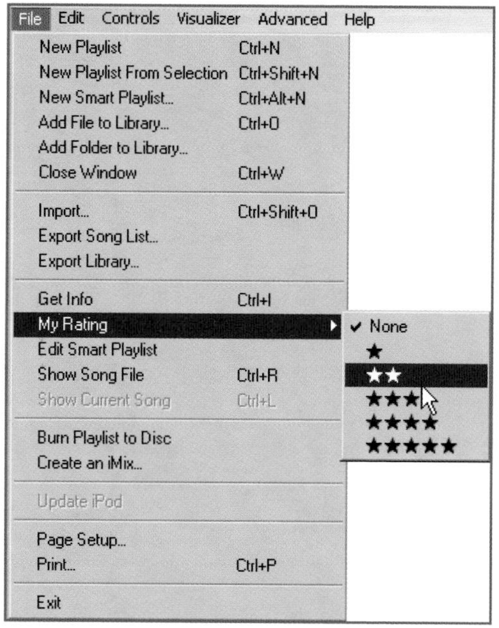

Figure 2-5: *You'll probably use the File menu mostly for creating different types of playlists.*

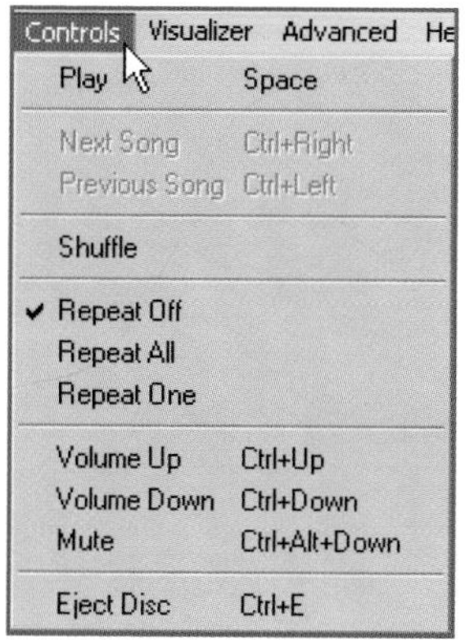

Figure 2-7: *If Apple could have left one menu out of the list, we suppose it'd be Controls.*

(clicking **Library** lists all your songs; clicking a **playlist** shows what's on it, and so on).

THE MENUS

As mentioned earlier, we're going to start using elements of the iTunes interface, but before we get down to the nitty-gritty, here's a short summation of the sorts of things you'll be able to do from each of the menus listed across the top of the iTunes window.

File

Here's where you create playlists and import music from folders on your hard drive, as well as do a lot of general messing around under iTunes' hood (Figure 2-5).

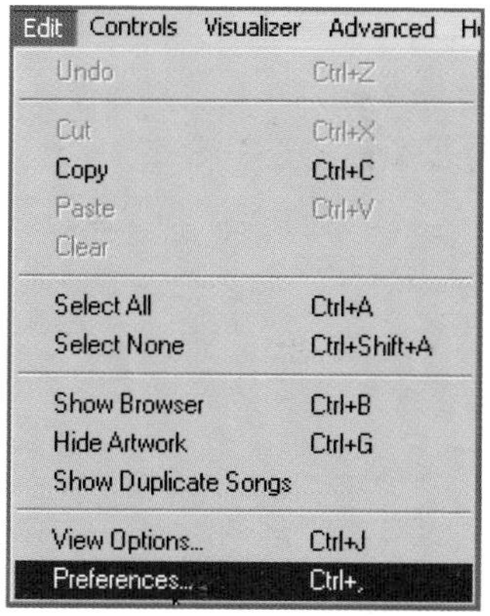

Edit

In the **Edit** menu (Figure 2-6), you can change the way iTunes displays things, edit your library, and alter **Preferences**—a menu item of ultimate importance when it comes to things like loading songs onto an iPod, importing or burning CDs, and sharing music between different computers on the same network.

Controls

We'd be willing to wager you won't use this menu much (Figure 2-7). There are better ways to control volume, fast forward, rewind, and shuffle. However, by looking at it you can pick up some useful keyboard shortcuts.

Figure 2-6: *The Preferences menu item is the most powerful feature in the Edit menu, according to four out of five dentists.*

Visualizer

If you want to turn your computer into a trippy light-show, this is the menu for you (Figure 2-8). Turn on the **Visualizer** and, once the **Visualizer** screen appears, tweak its few options by clicking the **Options** icon at the upper right. No, your mind isn't playing tricks on you—iTunes really does sync the graphics up with the music.

Advanced

The **Advanced** menu is actually more of a catch-all than a bunch of terribly advanced options. The one you'll probably make most use of is **Switch To Mini Player**; click this and iTunes morphs into a diminutive version of itself, which is handy for preserving screen space.

Figure 2-8: *Broadcast iTunes' Visualizer graphics onto the side of your garage with an LCD projector as iTunes syncs up the visuals with Pink Floyd's* Dark Side of the Moon—*you could probably charge admission.*

At this point, there's not much you need to know about checking for purchased music (Figure 2-9), but it will come in especially handy if you decide to upgrade to a different machine and want to transfer music you've purchased from the iTunes Music Store onto your new machine. (iTunes lets you keep songs you've purchased from iTunes on up to three computers.) **Consolidate Library** can also be helpful in such a situation. It copies any songs that exist outside your iTunes folder (leaving the originals where they are). This option can make it easy to transfer your whole library without missing anything.

As for some of the other **Advanced** menu options: **Open Stream** is for listening to streaming music—that is, music broadcast over the Internet. To listen to a stream just copy or type the web address, or "URL," into the dialog box that appears when you click **Open Stream**.

Click **Get CD Track Names** to prompt iTunes to check for album details in Gracenote's CDDB massive database of music data. Since it's impossible to have everything, don't be surprised if your album's information doesn't pop up. In that case you're stuck typing in song titles—but you can share your efforts by clicking **Submit CD Track Names**, which will send what you've typed to CDDB.

Figure 2-9: *Unlike some other online music stores, the Music Store aspect of iTunes makes it relatively easy to move your purchased tunes to a new computer.*

QUICKFACTS

SELECTING RIPPING SERVICES

Staring at your stack of CDs you might be wondering how you're going to rip through it and get all of those songs onto your computer (and from there to your iPod). If you've got more cash than free time, you should know that a cottage industry of rippers-for-hire has sprung up as millions of new iPod owners face the same hurdle. Most of these services cost about $1 per CD but vary based on volume. Is it worth it for you? Only you can balance the money versus time equation. Look in your local free papers or check out one of these websites, listed in alphabetical order:

- DMP3Music.com
- GetDigitalInc.com
- LoadPod.com
- RipDigital.com

Each of these has its own distinct advantages, so research them, as well as other services that might exist in your area, before deciding to send your CDs to someone for encoding.

Convert Selection To MP3 does just that—if a song is on a CD or in another format it will import it into iTunes as an MP3 file. This makes it possible to listen to it on a player that doesn't support AAC, for instance.

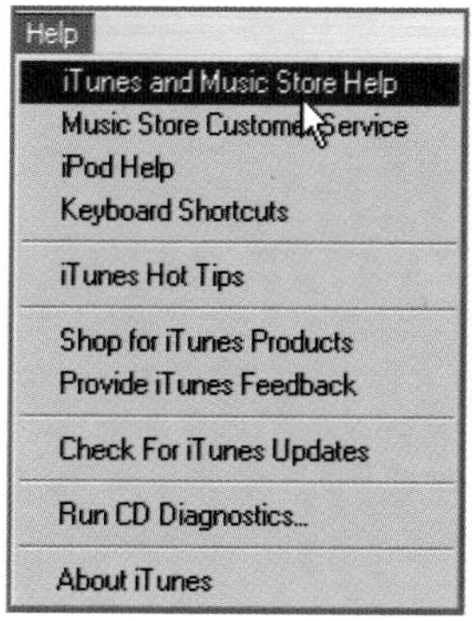

Figure 2-10: "Help" isn't just a four-letter word.

Help

Hey, what do you need this for? You already bought this book! Kidding aside, the **Help** menu (Figure 2-10) can come in handy when troubleshooting specific hardware problems, looking for upgrades, and learning keyboard shortcuts.

Get Music into iTunes

Whether you're new to digital music or already have a collection of digital music stored on your computer, you'll find the information you need in this section to get your music into iTunes. In the case of CDs, this is a matter of *importing* them (Apple's term for "ripping") onto your hard drive and encoding them into one of several compressed formats. We'll tackle importing an existing digital music collection consisting of files already stored on your computer later.

Understand Digital Audio File Types

Before we get into the business of ripping your CDs, you should know a few basics about the technology of digital music. While the reasonable default settings of iTunes mean that you can probably get by without knowing much of this, a little understanding of what digital music files are and how they differ from each other will help you best decide what you should be using.

RIP AND ENCODE (A.K.A. IMPORT FROM CD)

Rippers such as iTunes work by taking the songs on your audio CDs and *encoding* them into another digital format. Because audio files contain so much information, encoding usually involves some kind of file compression, which fits many more songs onto your computer and iPod drives than would be possible with songs at their original size. Of course, something is usually lost in the shrinking process; the key issue is whether or not you notice it's gone.

Uncompressed sound files contain much sonic data that not even the best-trained ears can register. Compression formulas work on the principle that if your ears don't notice something, it doesn't need to be there. Using formulas based on *psycho-acoustic modeling*, researchers have found a way to closely map what most people notice when they listen to music. That way, extraneous information can be tossed from a file. The accuracy of the psycho-acoustic model itself and how strongly it's applied make a big difference in how a compressed song sounds.

The MP3 format was the first of these compression schemes to really take hold on a large scale, and through popularity it became the default. Other companies and groups have created their own compression schemes, and the choice you get from iTunes represents Apple's picks of what's most useful for you and most convenient for its purposes, leaving you with a range of settings that can result in vastly different sound qualities. That's useful because different audio types suit different purposes.

COMPREHEND BIT RATE

Bit rate is an easy but important concept to understand because it has as much to do with sound quality as file type. Measured as bits per second, it tells you how many pieces of information are encoded for each second of a sound file; the higher the number, the more accurate the sound. One nice feature of iTunes is the ability to encode MP3 using VBR, or variable bit rate. That means that the program analyzes each section, or "frame," of sound and uses the optimal bit rate for each frame so the bit rate changes throughout the song as needed, depending on the sonic complexity of each passage. This helps keep file sizes lower and sound quality high—but even with this option, you can dictate the balance between sound quality and file size.

> ### NOTE
>
> As if this weren't confusing enough already, there's one more thing to consider: even within the same file type, there are different *codecs*, or *compression/ decompression algorithms*. Don't worry if it sounds too complicated; with iTunes, all of this takes place behind the scenes (but we'll show you how to tweak settings in a bit).

SETTING IMPORT PREFERENCES

Now it's finally time to decide which file format and bit rate you wish to use when turning your CDs into digital music files. Choose wisely; but on the other hand, remember that you can always change this setting later, if needed.

1. Click the **Edit** menu and select **Preferences**.

2. Under the **General** tab, make sure that **Connect To Internet When Needed** is checked.

3. Click the **Importing** tab. Choosing your preferences for importing can make a big difference in both sound quality and file size.

4. Choose your file type from the **Import Using** drop-down menu. The file type you choose affects how easily your music collection will work in players outside of iPod and iTunes. If you're planning on staying with the iPod/iTunes setup forever, as many are, go with **AAC Encoder**. For compatibility with other devices, pick **MP3 Encoder**.

5. From the **Setting** drop-down list, pick the bit rate. Choose **Custom Details**, if necessary, and a dialog box will pop up on which you can choose the settings you want. When in doubt, keep the entry fields at their default settings or **Auto**.

6. Check the **Play Songs While Importing** box if you want to hear the songs as you import them. Listening to music is what this is all about, but because encoding a song is much faster than listening to it, using this method will take a lot longer to rip your

Continued . . .

IMPORT FILE TYPES FOR iTUNES

Now that we've covered the different aspects of digital music files, let's take a look at the different file types iTunes can make out of your CDs.

- **AAC**   This is the file type that Apple stands behind, the one it uses for songs sold in the iTunes Music Store. It is a further evolution of the MP3 codec and was developed by Dolby, the same folks who work on surround sound and popularized noise reduction on cassette tapes; it offers superior sound quality at lower bit rates than MP3 does. It's less widely supported than MP3, potentially a drawback, but it certainly works well with all things iPod.

- **MP3**   The old standby offers good sound quality, particularly at higher bit rates, and iTunes' implementation lets you choose VBR (not an option under AAC). But the main advantage of MP3 is its nearly universal acceptance. Whether you choose AAC or MP3 probably depends on if you expect to use your music files in other programs.

- **AIFF**   This is an uncompressed file format, usually associated with Mac machines. It's basically the pure, extracted (and big!) file from a CD.

- **WAV**   This is an uncompressed file format, usually associated with Windows machines. Like AIFF, it's basically the pure, extracted (and big!) file from a CD.

- **Apple Lossless Encoder**   AAC and MP3 use *lossy* compression, meaning that no matter how good it sounds, some information is discarded in the process of shrinking the file. *Lossless* compression, on the other hand, shrinks a file by about half without losing any data. This 50 percent shrinkage ratio is nowhere near that of lossy formats, but lossless's advantage is that it retains every bit of audio information. Apple Lossless Encoder is Apple's proprietary lossless format and is good for making copies of anything where very high audio fidelity is necessary, since it sounds exactly as good as the original CD yet takes up half the space of a WAV or AIFF. If you're dumping your CDs to clean out your small apartment, this could be a good way to go to preserve them in the highest possible quality. If you're an audiophile, however, and value sound quality above disk space, lossless is the only way to go.

SELECT BIT RATES

Different file types offer you different choices for bit rates. The main thing to keep in mind is that the higher the bit rate, the better the sound and the bigger the file. Ideally, you should discover the point at which you can no longer tell

SETTING IMPORT PREFERENCES

(*Continued*)

songs. Unchecked is probably best when you start to import your collection. After that, when you get a new CD, check this so you can enjoy it as you import to iTunes.

7. Check the **Use Error Correction When Reading Audio CDs** box. This is a new, useful function if you have old, scratched, or dirty discs. The program will check to see if there are any errors reading your CD, and if so, will attempt to read it again to get it right. This slows things down considerably, so this option is best reserved for those times you need it.

That's it for settings. Back in the main screen, look to see if you're viewing the CD information. The name of the album and a CD icon should be outlined in the **Source** menu on the left; if not, click to select it.

a meaningful difference between the compressed song and the original. Then you can use that bit rate as your personal default and go up or down depending on the quality needed. For instance, if you're encoding spoken word, you don't need nearly as much fidelity as you do with a piece of chamber music.

SELECT VBR OPTIONS

If you decide to use VBR, you still have some choices to make. Instead of remaining constant, the settings you choose for bit rate become the guaranteed minimum quality. To get the full benefit that variability brings to file sizes, you should choose something lower than your normal bit rate preference here. The **Quality** setting gives iTunes an idea of where to set this when judging which bit rate to use for a particular frame.

Import CDs into iTunes

If you already have digital music on your computer, you should be able to load the songs into iTunes and by extension onto your iPod, so long as they're stored in any popular format aside from Windows Media (WMA), which is protected by digital rights management (DRM). If you have a bunch of CDs, iTunes will convert, or "import," that music. Don't have anything but a computer and your iPod? Well, as long as you've got an Internet connection and a credit card, iTunes is ready to help you develop a serious music habit. Don't even have a credit card? Don't lose hope! There are several legal free sites out that there that have some good music for most tastes (more on that in Chapter 9).

Add Your Existing Music Files to the iTunes Library

If you already have a collection of digital music files on your computer, you're probably itching to import those into iTunes. Relax; this is the easy part, if your files are in a compatible format (not WMA).

Before you start importing them, there's one thing you'll need to take care of first. If you have some stray files lying around, take this moment to organize them into a folder. If you don't want to do that, you can click **File** | **Add File To**

IMPORTING SONGS FROM CD TO iTUNES

Everything's squared away. Time to turn those CDs into digital music files for iTunes and (yes!) your iPod:

1. Make sure your settings are as you want them. (See the earlier sidebar "Setting Import Preferences.")

2. All songs on a CD are checked by default. The checkmark should be visible in a box just to the left of every song. Uncheck any songs you don't want.

3. Click the **Import** icon at the top right of the screen. It will change colors as the checked songs are imported. The **info** bar at the top lets you know which song is being imported and how far along the process is.

4. Wait for the ripping to finish. The speed depends mostly on two factors: your CD player and the processing power of your computer. Encoding is massive number crunching, and a strong CPU comes in very handy.

5. That's it. You've now imported your first songs. Relax and take a listen, or forge ahead with the rest of your collection.

TIP

You can also import files or folders to the iTunes Library using drag-and-drop. Just select **Library** in the **Source** pane and, outside of iTunes, click the folder or file you want to add and drag it over to the center iTunes pane. Your files will be added automatically.

Library to import single files, just as in the sidebar "Importing Songs from CD to iTunes." Then import your existing collection into iTunes:

1. Start iTunes, either by clicking your desktop shortcut or via the **Start** menu.

2. Decide whether you want to make a copy of all your music in the iTunes folder. This is convenient (if potentially confusing) for keeping all your music together. On the other hand, keeping doubles of relatively large music files wastes your hard drive space. If you do want this option, select **Edit | Preferences**, select the **Advanced** tab, and check **Copy Files To iTunes Music Folder When Adding To Library**. Close the **Preferences** dialog box.

3. Click **File | Add Folder To Library**.

4. In the dialog box that pops up, navigate to the folder with your music and click **OK** (Figure 2-11). This can be the highest-level folder you want—iTunes will import the contents of all lower-level folders contained within.

5. You'll see a pop-up box that shows the files of all your tunes being added.

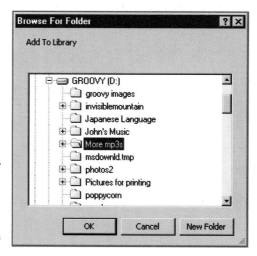

*Figure 2-11: **Navigate to the highest-level folder containing the songs you want to import.***

WHAT ABOUT WMA FILES?

If you've ripped a bunch of CDs in WMA and are hoping to use them with iTunes and iPod, it's not difficult. iTunes will import a WMA file and convert it to MP3 as long as it does not include any digital rights management (DRM). (The difference in copyright protection methods is one front in the cold war between Apple and Microsoft, so neither side's scheme works with the other's.) If you do have rights-protected files and they allow CD burning, you can make CDs and then reimport them. That solution's not the best for sound quality or time, but it's better than nothing.

USING COMPATIBLE FILE TYPES

iTunes and the iPod are compatible with a wide range of file types. In fact, the ability to use so many, particularly MP3, was one of the ways Apple convinced users from the shadowy world of anonymous MP3 trading to give the more restrictive world of iTunes a try. If they couldn't have imported their libraries of songs—however they got them—and transferred them onto the iPod, they probably wouldn't have given Apple a second thought.

Here's a list of audio file types compatible with iTunes and iPod by default.

- AAC
- Apple Lossless Encoder
- MP3
- MP3 VBR
- Protected AAC (using FairPlay)
- Audible
- WAV
- AIFF (except for the iPod Shuffle, which does not support AIFF)

(With third-party add-ons it's possible to expand iTunes compatibility with other file types, but be careful: just because one of these files plays on iTunes doesn't necessarily mean it will work on your iPod, which supports only MP3, AAC, WAV, AIFF, Apple Lossless, and Audible files.)

NOTE

If you choose to rip your CDs to AAC, the files you create will be different from AACs purchased from the iTunes Music Store, in that they are not restricted by the DRM rules specified later in this chapter.

As long as the unprotected WMA files are in the folders you specify for importing, iTunes will ask you whether you want them converted or not. This could take a while if you have a lot of WMA files. If your computer is maxed out with WMA files, you might have to convert them in batches (one folder at a time) and then delete the original WMA files.

AAC OR MP3?

There is a running debate between digital music mavens about which is better, AAC or MP3, and you can always find impassioned believers on either side. What you need to know is this: MP3 is over ten years old, and AAC is its successor. It's generally acknowledged that AAC files sound better than MP3s of the equivalent bit rate. The main tradeoff is that MP3 files are compatible with a wider rage of hardware and software (Apple and RCA are among the few hardware manufacturers that support AAC).

We hate to discourage anyone from geeking out and spending their days conducting quality tests, but before you lose any sleep, consider this reality check: MP3 and AAC are both pretty amazing, neither is perfect, and you'll probably spend your time much more enjoyably listening to your music than puzzling over which format to go with. Doubt that? Ask a friend to help you blindly compare a few files. Then pick one and stick with it.

ADD ALBUM ART

If you buy a track from iTunes Music Store, it will come with album art attached. For other sources, if you want art, you'll need to find and add it yourself. This is one method for adding album covers to songs you've already imported:

1. Select all tracks from an album.
2. Right-click the selected tracks.
3. Use your web browser to find a source for album art. (Hint: you might try the big online store from which you purchased your CD.)
4. Drag and drop the album art from your web browser into the **album art** pane in the iTunes dialog box (Figure 2-12).

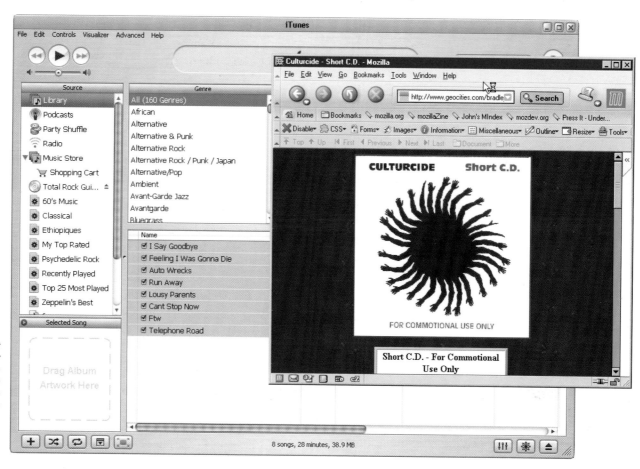

Figure 2-12: *You might need to make your browser small enough that you can still see iTunes well enough to drop the album art into the right place.*

5. An information box will pop up letting you know the artwork is being loaded. Because the image has to be added to each file, this can take a while.

Album artwork has now been added and should appear in the **Selected Song** pane. Click in that pane for a new window to open and display the art full size (Figure 2-13). For those rare CDs that don't have an online picture, you'll need to scan that art and resize it yourself. This is another reason to get your pile of music ripped by a service: most of them add artwork as well.

*Figure 2-13: **Click the displayed artwork to show the image at full resolution in a separate window.***

Visit Music Stores

Ever since music met the Internet to form digital music, people have been talking about their intense relationship to that combination of forces. Sure, we've had our spats (certain lawsuits spring to mind), but that's normal—especially for couples who as feel as threatened by each other as music labels and fans of music technology sometimes do.

Shop at the iTunes Music Store

Apple mastermind Steve Jobs was the first technology guy to convince the major labels to license their music for sale online on any scale that mattered. Chalk it up to his charisma, his sympathetic ties to movie production house Pixar, or the fact that the record labels saw the (initially) Mac-only iTunes Music Store as a safe way to test the waters before rolling it out to the mainstream Windows market. The point remains that Jobs' iTunes Music Store was the first digital music store to make some degree of sense to music labels, music fans, and a technology company.

iTunes continues to be a popular place for music fans, and iPod owners in particular, to buy music. Prices for songs and albums at the time this book went to print were $0.99 and $9.99, respectively.

SIGN INTO THE iTUNES MUSIC STORE

Before you can buy songs from the iTunes Music Store, you'll need to fork over some personal info and your credit card information. Don't worry—you won't be charged for anything until you buy a song, which requires a confirmation step. Click the **Account: Sign In** button near the upper-right corner of iTunes (Figure 2-14).

CREATE A NEW ACCOUNT

If you already have an account with Apple (a strong possibility if you've registered other products from them) enter your Apple ID, which is usually an

Figure 2-14: *Even if you were already shopping at iTunes Music Store before you bought your iPod, you still have to sign in.*

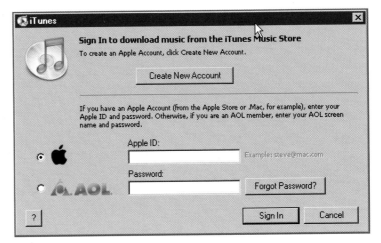

QUICKFACTS

SHOPPING AT OTHER ONLINE DIGITAL MUSIC STORES

Apple's iTunes Music Store is the easiest place to buy music for your iPod, since the storefront's right inside of iTunes. But you can also buy from these other stores, which sell songs in iPod-compatible formats (import them into iTunes using the directions given earlier in this chapter).

- **EMusic**   Subscribe to this service for 10 bucks a month, and you'll get 40 unrestricted MP3s a month.

- **AudioLunchbox.com**   Buy music from independent artists in the MP3 format at a 192Kbps bit rate.

- **Bleep.com**   If you're into electronic music, browse this site for high-quality downloads.

- **Garageband.com**   As its name suggests, this site is a good place to find music from mostly unsigned bands, some of it free and some of it for a charge.

- **MP3.com**   This site lets you search and download from the iTunes Music Store and some of the other iPod-compatible services enumerated in the rest of this list from one search box. (Full disclosure: Eliot Van Buskirk, one of the authors of this book, is technology editor for MP3.com.)

- **MP3Tunes.com**   Buy unrestricted MP3s from this site via the Web.

- **Music.download.com**   Download free tracks from a variety of artists and labels in the MP3 format. (Note: CNET owns both MP3.com and Music .download.com.)

e-mail address, and your password. If you don't already have an account with Apple or if you want to start a new one anyway, click the **Create New Account** button (Figure 2-15).

Figure 2-15: *Once you create this account, buying songs through iTunes is a snap.*

Terms of Service

Click that you agree to the Terms of Service—if you agree, that is; if not, we recommend that you buy your music on CDs instead and import them into iTunes using the instructions later in this chapter.

Create an Apple Account

Follow the instructions and click the **Continue** button at the lower right once you've filled out the boxes and checked off the appropriate checkboxes for whatever mailings you might wish to receive.

Credit Card Time

You know what to do here. For information on the potential risks of sending your credit card information over the Internet to Apple's servers, please see the QuickFacts sidebar "Credit Card Security."

QUICKFACTS

CREDIT CARD SECURITY

If you're a veteran of buying stuff on the Internet, you know it's always a good idea—rather, a prerequisite—to know that you're submitting your credit card information to a secure party in a secure way. Here are some quick facts about credit card security as it concerns buying digital music from the iTunes Music Store and other sources.

- We started covering digital music before iTunes was released and have yet to hear of anyone having their credit card data swiped due to buying songs from reputable online music stores such as iTunes.

- The standard precautions apply: use a firewall and an appropriate level of security on your wireless network, if you have one.

- Once you enter your information, you'll be able to sign in from up to three other computers.

CAUTION

If you see an e-mail or online ad for "100% Free, Legal Downloads" with an offer to download as much music and film and as many video games as you want for a lifetime membership for a monthly rate that seems too good to be true, it is. Don't sign up; they're offering you access to file sharing networks that are free to use and offer no legal defense against accusations of copyright infringement.

Congratulations! Assuming your credit card was accepted, you'll now be able to buy songs with one click (generally) from anywhere within the 1.5 million songs and growing iTunes Music Store.

DRM RESTRICTIONS ON SONGS PURCHASED FROM iTUNES

The files that you buy from the iTunes Music Store come with DRM (digital rights management) technology. Apple's copyright protection is called FairPlay. Apple occasionally changes the rules that apply to these songs as part of the continuing negotiations between Apple and the record labels that own the music it sells on its store. Copyright protection such as FairPlay is the reason some people prefer to buy their music on CD—that way, you can use the CD as a source and turn it into whichever file types your home and portable devices can play, whether they're from Apple or some other manufacturer. Here's what the restrictions are right now:

- The songs you purchase will play only on your iPods and up to five computers. This is to prevent you from granting a large group of freeloading friends full access to your digital music.

- You can only burn the same playlist to CD-R ten times. You can still, however, burn all of those songs in a new playlist. This rule exists to thwart would-be pirates from using iTunes Music Store and its burning capabilities to create bootleg CD-Rs for sale on the street, eBay, or any number of other places.

- The files will only play back in iTunes or on an iPod. Real, the creator of the RealPlayer software and Real Rhapsody online music service, has tried to enable their songs to play on iPods as well but have been met with resistance by Apple. If you plan on using only iPods for your portable listening, your iTunes-running computer(s), or the Airport Express iTunes-to-stereo device (which we'll get to in Chapter 8), these restrictions won't bother you.

The Ins and Outs of Buying Digital Music

Now you should see the interface of the iTunes Music Store, as you did back before you signed in. The only difference visually is that at the upper right, you'll see your account name (also known as your Apple ID—the e-mail address you set up earlier in this section).

NOTE

You have to be online to shop at the iTunes Music Store. The faster your connection, the more pleasant your shopping experience will be.

There are a number of ways to find songs and albums for purchase in the iTunes Music Store. It has its disadvantages compared to a real record store with a knowledgeable staff and albums that you can actually pick up and hold. (But if the record stores around where you live don't have knowledgeable staff on hand, it's not worth asking for recommendations anyway.)

One nice thing about the iTunes Music Store is the sheer number of ways it offers for discovering new music. Try poking around and searching—you might be surprised by the breadth of what's available. Here are a few of the ways in which you can discover music (Figure 2-16), from searching to browsing to celebrity recommendations.

Figure 2-16: The front of the iTunes Music Store presents music in an increasingly wide variety of ways. As you'll notice, the Search box at the upper right now says Search Music Store. If you know what you want, that's where to start.

Browsing the store is a lot like surfing the Web—you just keep clicking around. To the upper left, you'll even notice buttons for **back**, **forward**, and **home**, just as in your web browser.

BUY A SONG ONLINE

Now that you've figured out how to browse around, perhaps you'd like to buy a song or two. It's quite simple:

1. Find a song you'd like to buy, either by browsing or searching, as described earlier.

2. Click the **Add Song** button to the right of the song in the **song listing** pane (Figure 2-17).

	Song Name	Time	Artist		Album	Price	
1	Only the Young	4:07	Journey	○	Journey: Greatest...	$0.99	ADD SONG
2	Don't Stop Believin'	4:08	Journey	○	Journey: Greatest...	$0.99	ADD SONG
3	Wheel in the Sky	4:14	Journey	○	Journey: Greatest...	$0.99	ADD SONG
4	Faithfully	4:26	Journey	○	Journey: Greatest...	$0.99	ADD SONG
5	I'll Be Alright Without You	4:50	Journey	○	Journey: Greatest...	$0.99	ADD SONG
6	Any Way You Want It	3:23	Journey	○	Journey: Greatest...	$0.99	ADD SONG
7	Ask the Lonely	3:54	Journey	○	Journey: Greatest...	$0.99	ADD SONG
8	Who's Crying Now	5:01	Journey	○	Journey: Greatest...	$0.99	ADD SONG
9	Separate Ways (Worlds Apart)	5:26	Journey	○	Journey: Greatest...	$0.99	ADD SONG
10	Lights	3:09	Journey	○	Journey: Greatest...	$0.99	ADD SONG
11	Lovin', Touchin', Squeezin'	3:51	Journey	○	Journey: Greatest...	$0.99	ADD SONG
12	Open Arms	3:19	Journey	○	Journey: Greatest...	$0.99	ADD SONG
13	Girl Can't Help It	3:50	Journey	○	Journey: Greatest...	$0.99	ADD SONG
14	Send Her My Love	3:55	Journey	○	Journey: Greatest...	$0.99	ADD SONG
15	Be Good to Yourself	3:51	Journey	○	Journey: Greatest...	$0.99	ADD SONG

Figure 2-17: *Easy enough—one click does it all.*

Figure 2-18: *Of course, you have to be connected to the Internet in order for this to work. After all, iTunes has to talk to Apple's servers, take your payment, and download the song to you.*

Figure 2-19: *You can watch the song's download progress in the bubble window at the top of the screen.*

3. iTunes will verify the purchase on the **info** bar—it only takes a few seconds with a fast broadband connection (Figure 2-18).

4. Now the downloading begins (Figure 2-19).

5. All the songs you purchase from the iTunes Music Store can be accessed by clicking **Purchased Songs** in the **Source** pane.

You'll see albums for sale in iTunes as well. Sometimes you can get a better deal buying albums—their $9.99 standard price often gives you more than ten songs, which usually go for $0.99 apiece.

Tune into Podcasts

The last two years have seen the podcast leap from being an obscure, nerdy obsession to being the latest online audio craze. (Note to music execs: pay more attention to nerds!)

Though it has a fancy name, a podcast is basically just a regular old audio file tied to some special Internet information that lets people, with the right program, subscribe to it. Now that program can be iTunes. Just like radio or TV, the premise is that the podcast creator will release new episodes at some time, predetermined or not, and alert subscribers to download them.

Starting with iTunes 4.9, Apple began including podcast functions. To make things simple podcasts were integrated with the iTunes store, so getting a podcast is now about as easy as picking out a new tune (Figure 2-20). In fact, since you don't have to worry about paying for most podcasts—it can be even easier than buying music.

Figure 2-20: Podcasts are now included as part of the iTunes store—we only wish more stores had this much stuff for free!

Apple's inclusion of podcast tools in iTunes has carried both public validation for the groundswell of listeners and producers, as well as a predictable push to promote more mainstream content as "podcasting" becomes a household word. Right now is probably the golden age of the format, when big names share space with anyone who has enough gumption to put a show together. Pretty powerful stuff, and just what all those prophets of computer age global empowerment predicted.

Because podcasting is an interesting new world that Apple has entered, we've included more descriptions and options in Chapters 4 and 9. For now, we'll give you enough information to get you up and running with one of the easiest ways going to fill up all 40 gigabytes of your new iPod, without dipping into any of those legally gray zones like file trading.

Chapter 3
Using Your iPod

It's doubtful you bought your iPod so that you could revel in the glories of iTunes, no matter how slick its interface or how great its features; chances are you wanted to carry your music with you, rocking out as you walk to work or relaxing on the bus ride home. Now the moment of truth has arrived: the hard work of loading your music to your library is done, and you're about to take your iPod for a spin. Hold your horses just a little, because you want to make sure to do it right.

The iPod is certainly a wonder of engineering. One of Apple's long-time strengths has been the ability to group together complex, edgy technologies in forms that make them deceptively simple and easy to use. The iPod is a product of this talent, and though it is remarkably intuitive to pick up and play with, that simplicity masks some powerful capabilities. This chapter will walk you through some of the basics.

MANUAL OR AUTOMATIC SYNCING?

For most people, automatic syncing is the way to go because it's easy, and it ensures your iPod gets filled with whatever new music you have in iTunes when you connect it. For those whose collection is larger than the capacity of their iPod—mainly Shuffle and Mini owners—and don't mind iTunes randomly adding and subtracting music from their iPod, then automatic is still a good call.

If you're not the type of person who likes surprises and you'd prefer total control over what's on your iPod, stick with one of the manual syncing options.

TIP

To rename your iPod at any time, left-click it once in the **Sources** pane, and then wait a couple of seconds. Click it again, and then start typing. You can call it anything you want, just don't call it late for . . . aw, forget it.

Execute One Full Automatic Sync

There are other library management issues that we'll deal with in other chapters, such as what to do if you need to change computers. For the purposes of starting out, we're going to assume that your total library of tunes isn't bigger than your iPod's capacity, and that automatic syncing is best for you. Let's get to it.

Use Basic Syncing Methods

For now, we'll concentrate on getting music from iTunes onto your iPod in the simplest way: autosynching. Directions for other methods, such as manual syncing, will follow quickly.

ACCESS iPOD OPTIONS

To get up and running, you first need to make sure your settings are as you want them.

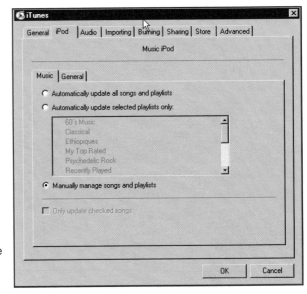

1. Connect your iPod to your computer, if it's not already connected. (If you skipped the part about connecting, please refer back to Chapter 1 and follow those directions, or iTunes won't recognize the iPod.)

2. Once it's recognized by iTunes, your iPod will show up in the **Sources** pane at the upper left. Right-click your iPod.

Figure 3-1: The iPod Options menu offers you choices about how to load music onto your iPod.

3. Select **iPod Options** from the pop-up menu and the **iTunes** dialog appears with the **iPod** tab selected (Figure 3-1). This is what Apple sometimes calls the "**iPod Options**" menu.

AUTOSYNC YOUR iTUNES LIBRARY TO YOUR iPOD

This is the easiest way to get music onto your iPod so you can get outside and enjoy that sunny day.

1. Open **iPod Options** (see the previous section).

2. Select **Automatically Update All Songs And Playlists** (another option in Figure 3-1).

3. Now whenever you connect your iPod, iTunes will automatically update it with any new songs you've added to your collection.

If your iTunes library contains more music than your iPod has room for, iTunes will pick a selection of songs from your library. For now, we recommend this option, although in Chapter 4, once you've built more playlists, you'll get into some more advanced methods of syncing, mentioned in the "Trying Other Syncing Options" QuickFacts module.

Work the Wheel

It'd take approximately 500,000 pages of raw ASCII text files to fill just 1 GB of the space on your iPod; this is about a third of the number of pages returned by Google today on a search for the term "iPod scroll wheel." (See the search results at the top of the next page.)

There's a good reason that so much has been written about the scroll wheel: as a design innovation it ranks high. The scroll wheel's circular design allows you to scroll continuously, unlike other touch-sensitive controls that force you to navigate in jumps (with the competition's touch strips, you have to return your thumb to the top of the control strip in order to scroll through another screen's worth of song titles). The iPod's scroll wheel, coupled with the way Apple designed the scrolling speed of long lists to accelerate through them, has been widely credited with the success of the iPod line.

Apple refined the wheel control on the iPod a few times on the way down the line. Here's how the latest design, the click wheel (found on the 4G iPod, iPod Mini, and iPod Photo) works. We discuss the various earlier iPod models at

more length in Chapter 1, and since the menu structure is the same for all iPods with screens, we'll just cover the click wheel here. Here's how it works.

Work the Click Wheel

The key thing you need to know about the click wheel is that it's both touch-sensitive and clickable. Whether you're right- or left-handed, lightly drag your thumb in a circle around the click wheel. That's scrolling. You can press the wheel in one of four directions to click it: up (**Menu**), down (**Play/Pause**), left (**Rewind**), and right (**Fast Forward**). Pretty simple—that's why the iPod's click wheel design has been such a big hit with consumers and tech critics alike.

BASIC CLICK WHEEL FUNCTIONS

The click wheel works differently on different screens, and we'll get into that soon. Here's what its six controls do, no matter which screen you're on.

WHAT IS FIRMWARE?

Your computer has an operating system that lets it run programs; you can upgrade it in order to add features, improve performance, and whatever else Apple or Microsoft wants to improve for a given model. Likewise, your iPod has a processor chip that can be similarly upgraded. Think of it as your iPod's brain, which you can rebuild if you have the technology. Your iPod's operating system is called "firmware" because as a technology, it's right in between hardware and software. The iPod Updater program on your installation CD and, now, on your computer, can update your iPod's firmware (no songs get deleted).

- Press and hold **Play/Pause**: turns the iPod off.
- Press and hold **Menu**: turns Backlight on/off.
- Press **Menu**: goes up one screen in the menu structure (if you select something and want to go back to where you were before you selected it, press **Menu**).
- Press and hold the **center** button and **Menu** simultaneously: resets the iPod (this is useful if your iPod freezes up, which should happen only very rarely).
- Scroll clockwise/counterclockwise: moves cursor up and down or sliders left and right.
- Press the **center** button: selects menu item.
- Press and hold the **center** button: special function (this one varies a lot, depending on context).

Poke around; you can't break the iPod with mere curiosity. Scroll to move the cursor, click the **center** button to select items, and use the **Menu** button to go back up a level or two. Here are some major points of interest on each screen of each iPod.

The Main Menu Screen

The various iPods' menus are fairly similar, but the 4G iPod and iPod Mini menus vary slightly, in that the Mini's screen is smaller. However, the screen appears just as sharp, because the dot pitch is smaller. In English, that means the screens can hold the same amount of text in a smaller area without losing clarity. This section covers everything on the 4G iPod and iPod Mini. As for the iPod Photo, it's pretty much the same except it has a color screen (Figure 3-2), and a few other menu items we'll explore in a bit. The Shuffle, of course, has no screen at all, and thus no menu.

‖	iPod	▭
Music		>
Photos		>
Extras		>
Settings		>
Shuffle Songs		>
Backlight		>

Figure 3-2: The iPod Main menu is basically the same on all iPods but the Shuffle.

Access Music

The **Music** menu lets you access the music on your iPod in a variety of ways. Browse around (this menu item was called **Browse** in previous firmware versions) the various categories (Figure 3-3). You might consider moving one or two of these. **Playlists**, **Albums**, and/or **Artists** can be handy to have on the **Main** menu screen rather than nested away in the **Music** area. To move them onto the **Main** menu, see the QuickSteps for "Customizing the Main Menu" in this section.

Figure 3-3: The Music menu is your most direct path to the music you want to hear.

Use the Extras

You'll find **Clock**, **Contacts**, **Calendar**, **Notes**, and **Games** in the **Extras** menu (Figure 3-4). You'll use these features later, but again, feel free to poke around. There are some optional items you might want to add using the following QuickSteps.

PHOTO IMPORT

This optional **Extra** menu item lets your 4G iPod or iPod Photo grab photos from most digital cameras, using an optional accessory we'll mention in Chapter 7.

Figure 3-4: The Extras menu offers all sorts of goodies that increase your iPod's functionality.

VOICE MEMOS

Another item you can choose to add to the **Extras** menu is the **Voice Memos** item, which allows direct access to memos recorded using another optional accessory.

QUICKSTEPS

CUSTOMIZING THE MAIN MENU

You can choose any item listed on the **Music** and **Extras** menus and have it included in the **Main** menu, or you can remove **Main** menu items you don't use much. This is easy, and well worth it, especially if there's something buried in one of the submenus that you find yourself accessing a lot. This is a nice feature to have because it keeps the default **Main** menu neat for those users who don't need to access those additional functions quickly, but lets those of us who want to, play around with the iPod's main screen.

1. Go into the **Settings** menu and select **Main Menu** from the list (it's the second one down).

2. To put whatever you want to include on the **Main** menu, scroll to the item to select it, and then click the **center** button so that selection is shown as being **On** (clicking again turns the item to the **Off** position and removes it from the **Main** menu).

3. To return the **Main** menu to its original state, just click **Menu** twice.

4. Repeat these steps to add as many menu items as you want; just don't pick them all, unless you want the **Main** menu to get cluttered up.

TIP

Don't freak out if your iPod occasionally takes a little longer between songs while playing. That's normal; it means that your iPod's hard drive is loading its RAM (temporary memory) with the next set of songs.

Set the Settings

Much of what you'll find here is self-explanatory, but here are a few key items on the **Settings** menu (Figure 3-5).

- **Main Menu**   We covered this in the QuickSteps; if you skipped it, it's worth a look.

- **EQ**   These settings process sound. Purists generally don't want to alter these settings, but even they'd have to admit that equalization can help some headphones and speakers— especially the ones they'd never own.

- **Sound Check**   Even if you get all of your music from the same source, there are bound to be differences in volume in the songs in your library, especially if you do a lot of shuffling. **Sound Check** evens these out, although in some people's opinions it doesn't do as good a job as normalizing software, or even iTunes' own sound leveling feature (see Chapter 4).

Figure 3-5: The Settings menu lets you tweak your iPod options, as well as make convenient changes to the interface.

Shuffle Songs

One of our personal favorites, this default Main menu item lets you cut right to the chase and start your whole iPod library playing at random (Figure 3-6). Hear a song you don't like? Hit **Fast Forward** and see what comes next. (This is the sort of thinking that inspired the iPod Shuffle.) Unlike many other MP3 players, the iPod remembers the last songs it shuffled from, so when you hit **Rewind** you can hear the last song(s) again; **Fast Forward** brings you back to the front of the randomly generated list.

Figure 3-6: Shuffle lets you surprise yourself with songs chosen randomly from your library.

FINDING A SPECIFIC SPOT IN A SONG

Skipping to any part of a song or audio book is easy, although truth be told, if you're just trying to fast forward or rewind a little bit, holding down **Fast Forward** or **Rewind** will get you there faster. (In the case of audio books, many include bookmarks anyway; click **Fast Forward** or **Rewind** to skip to one of them.)

1. If you're not already there, go to the **Now Playing** screen.
2. Tap the **center** button once.
3. Scroll to the right or left in order to pick a new spot to start from.
4. Tap the **center** button again and the song will pick up from the new spot.

NOTE

You can only have one On-the-Go playlist on your iPod at a time, but you can save them in iTunes for later use (we'll show you how in Chapter 4).

Turn on Backlight

The **Backlight Main** menu item toggles the iPod's backlight on and off. It's not quite bright enough to use in a pinch as a flashlight, although the iPod Photo comes closer. The backlight will stay on for as many seconds as you specify in the **Settings** menu, or even permanently (or at least until the battery needs to be recharged again).

View Now Playing

This item only shows up when a song is playing, or when a song is paused. It takes you back to the **Now Playing** screen, as you would imagine (Figure 3-7). Here, you'll mainly change volume with the scroll wheel, read song information, check out album art (iPod Photo only), and rate songs (see the QuickSteps sidebar later in this chapter).

Figure 3-7: The Now Playing screen lets you know what you're hearing (to access it quickly from most screens, scroll down all the way and click the center button).

Create an On-the-Go Playlist on Your iPod

We'll get to creating playlists in iTunes in the next chapter, but as long as we're talking about the iPod on its own, we'd be remiss if we didn't mention On-the-Go playlists. You pick songs one after the other, and they play in that order. It's like having a jukebox in your pocket, except you don't have to pay to play the songs and you can fast forward and rewind. This is a great way to pick a spontaneous set of as many songs as you want (on all iPods except for the Shuffle line).

1. Go to the **Main** menu screen.
2. Scroll to **Music** and click the **center** button.
3. If you want to add entire albums, click **Album** with the **center** button; or, to add everything from a band or solo artist, click **Artist**. If you want to build your On-the-Go playlist song-by-song, chose **Songs**.

QUICKSTEPS

DEALING WITH VOLUME

One drawback to the iPod's clean, click wheel–based approach is that if you're not on the **Now Playing** screen, you can't adjust volume quickly. Most of the time this isn't a problem, but if, say, you suddenly get to the front of the line at the QuickyMart and you're deep into some menu or another, you'll need a quick way to adjust volume. For an instant solution, click the **Play/Pause** button. Or follow these steps to reduce volume (there are accessories that can do this more quickly in Chapter 7; Apple's own line-in remote control can do it too).

1. Click **Menu** until you're at the **Main** menu screen.

2. Scroll the click wheel in a quick clockwise circle— you're trying to scroll all the way down the list to the **Now Playing** menu item, which is at the bottom of the list (good thinking on Apple's part to facilitate at least this quick workaround for getting to the volume control quickly).

3. Click the **center** button.

4. Scroll the click wheel to the left to turn volume down (right volume to turn it up—helpful if you're not in the front of the line yet, and someone behind you is blabbing on a cell phone).

5. This took awhile. See why we recommended hitting **Pause** instead when you're in the QuickyMart? **Pause** works from any menu screen.

4. To add a song, album, or artist, scroll to it and hold down the **center** button until you see a title or artist name blink. You just added it to the On-the-Go playlist.

5. Repeat this process, browsing around for whatever you want to hear, in the order in which you want to hear it. Remember, **Menu** functions as a **Back** button when you're browsing; use it to switch between adding songs, artists, and albums.

6. When you're satisfied with your list (you can always add to it later), click the **Menu** button until you return to the **Main** menu.

7. To play the On-the-Go playlist you just created, click **Music | Playlists** and scroll down to **On-The-Go** (Figure 3-8). Click the **Play/Pause** button on the click wheel—don't click the **center** button, or you'll start browsing the playlist (which is fine if you want to start from the middle of the set, but a waste of a click if you just want to start listening).

8. If you want to clear the whole On-the-Go playlist, scroll down within it and click **Clear**.

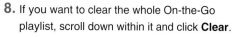

II	Playlists	🔋
On-The-Go		>

Figure 3-8: An On-The-Go playlist is a handy way to play your songs jukebox style.

Add Photos to the iPod

1. Connect your iPod to your computer (iPod Shuffle excluded).

2. Click the iPod **Options** icon in the lower right of the iTunes screen. The **Preferences** dialog box will open.

3. Under the **Photos** tab check **Synchronize Photos From**, which is followed by a drop-down menu. In Windows machines your **My Pictures** folder will be automatically selected. If you want a different folder scroll down to pick **Choose Folder**.

4. Choose either **Copy All Photos** or **Copy Selected Folders Only** (Figure 3-9).

5. If you chose the **Copy Selected Folders Only** option, choose the folder you wish to import.

6. iTunes will create smaller versions of your photos to import for display on your iPod.

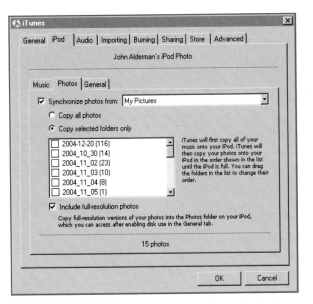

Figure 3-9: In typical Apple fashion, dealing with photos on the iPod is a lot easier and simpler than it could be.

From the same dialog box, you may also choose to include photos at full resolution. Since this is mainly for displaying at high resolutions when hooked up to TVs, you should probably leave this off for now. Don't worry, we'll cover this further in Chapter 6.

The iPod's color screen was designed for photos, but it adds a few other cool features, such as the ability to see full-color artwork (usually album art) as a song plays. In order to view album art on your iPod, make sure to check **Display Album Artwork** in your iPod, under the **iPod | Music** in **iPod Options**. (For adding artwork to songs, see our instructions in Chapter 2.)

Use the iPod Shuffle

The entire iPod line is known for its simplicity of use, but the Shuffle takes this concept to an extreme. It lacks a screen and wheel control, but as you know if you've ever seen an ad for the device, it's not designed with playlists, albums, and other set forms of playback. As the name implies, it's for shuffling, or letting your music play randomly.

This doesn't mean that the Shuffle can't use a playlist; it can, but in a different way than other iPods. To keep things simple, the Shuffle uses only one internal list. To edit that list, or to switch to other lists as sources for importing music, you'll need to rely on iTunes.

In the QuickSteps sidebar, you'll find instructions for the most basic way of importing tunes into the Shuffle; it's quick and random.

It's that easy. If you'd like to import from a particular playlist, you can choose that list as your source by choosing **Autofill** from the drop-down menu. If a list of songs is bigger than your iPod you can still use it as the playlist, but it will stop when the memory is full. You can set whether iTunes chooses songs randomly or from the top down in order.

SYNCING MUSIC TO THE iPOD SHUFFLE AUTOMATICALLY

1. Remove the USB cap or lanyard from the Shuffle and plug it in to your computer's USB port.

2. Choose your iPod in the **Source** pane.

3. Click the **Autofill** button now displayed underneath the track listing, as shown here.

4. iTunes will randomly choose songs from your library and fill your Shuffle, according to the default settings.

This pulls songs in at random and makes a basic internal playlist of songs. The order of playback from that list depends on the control settings on the iPod itself. On the back switch you have the choice of playing in the order the songs were imported or at random.

TIP

You don't need to worry as much about the battery in your iPod Shuffle. The Shuffle's battery is smaller, but since it has no moving parts (songs are stored on flash memory rather than a hard drive), it lasts a lot longer.

Manage iPod Battery Life: a Balancing Act

If there's one major weakness with the iPod it's the battery. Many iPod competitors, for all their faults, simply stay charged longer. The fact that the battery is not intended to be user replaceable, an attribute shared with most—but not all—other players, is also a drawback. In its favor, Apple has consistently worked to improve battery life and has always done a good job of striking a winning balance between form and function. Despite good improvements with the most recent generation, for the iPod owner, battery life remains a subject of concern.

As with mobile phones, digital cameras, and many other portable electronic devices, the iPod's battery is conveniently rechargeable lithium ion. These batteries are wonderful in many ways, and the iPod's designers did a remarkable job of integrating power source and hard disk in such a small package. You can spend the day running around listening to music, and instead of having to run to your convenience store every night to pick up batteries, you can simply hook up the iPod to a power source and it's ready to go in the morning. This blissful existence doesn't last forever, though, and after a period of usually about two or three years, the battery's ability to retain a charge wears off. When this happens you'll need to replace it. (For advice on replacing the battery turn to Chapter 10.)

Meanwhile, when it comes to the iPod battery, the most pressing concerns for users are how to get the most bang per charge and how to extend battery life. To this end, it's best to understand a little bit about how the iPod works.

QUICKSTEPS

RATING SONGS ON THE iPOD

You can rate the currently playing song at any time. Almost all song listings contain a **Rating** column; just click there to rate one. Later, when you're creating Smart Playlists, you can use these ratings to create your own sets of greatest hits.

1. If you're not already there, go to the **Now Playing** screen.

2. If you're near the end of the song, click **Pause** so that your iPod doesn't get to the next song before you rate this one.

3. Tap the **center** button twice.

4. You'll see five dots in a horizontal line; scroll to the right or left in order to rate the currently playing song, from 1 to 5 stars.

5. The next time you connect your iPod to your computer, these ratings will get stored and displayed in iTunes. They'll come into play when we talk about Smart Playlists in Chapter 4.

How Playing Songs Drains Energy

In order to play sounds, the iPod's chip draws song data from the hard disk in large chunks and then keeps that information in memory (a chip of RAM, similar to the memory your computer uses). Having enough song data in memory provides a buffer, and any bumps to the drive or other hiccups don't result in any interruptions to your listening pleasure. The hard drive is the largest user of energy out of all the iPod's components.

Because of how that data buffering is done, it saves your charge if you make a playlist and stick with it, rather that skipping around from song to song. Otherwise the iPod draws data that it doesn't use, spinning the hard disk more frequently. Of course, if you're tired of hearing a song, don't torture yourself on account of battery life. But a little planning lets you not only play DJ to your life, but also keeps your iPod going longer.

Tips for Battery Use

Again, you needn't get too worked up about battery life; even if you don't heed any of this advice, it'll retain a decent battery life for at least two years, at which point you can have it replaced, if you so desire. That said, there a few more things to keep in mind.

TRY TO USE ALL OF EACH CHARGE

The iPod's battery dies when it reaches a certain number of charges, so the less often you charge it, the longer it'll stay able to hold a charge. That means you should try to let the battery bar run itself all the way down when convenient, rather than charging it when it doesn't really need the juice.

MAKE SURE YOUR FIRMWARE IS UPDATED

Because Apple works to increase the efficiency of the iPod software, making sure that you have the latest update can mean a big improvement in battery life. See the QuickSteps sidebar for how to update.

QUICKSTEPS

UPDATING YOUR iPOD'S FIRMWARE

If your iPod's brand new, there's a good chance that you don't have to deal with this right now. But you might have bought a model that was built and shipped before an update was released, and in any case you should update your player's firmware periodically.

1. Connect your computer to the Internet (if you have broadband, as we recommend, it's probably already connected).

2. Connect your iPod to your computer.

3. Go to **Start** | **All Programs** | **iPod** | **iPod Updater 20xx-xx-xx** (it'll have the date Apple released it in the title).

4. Run **iPod Updater**.

If you try to update your iPod's firmware and get an error message, chances are that means you need to go to apple.com/ipod/download and get the latest version of the iPod Updater software.

TURN OUT THE LIGHTS

The backlight can use a lot of energy, so if you're concerned, use the **Settings** menu on the iPod to change **Backlight Timer** to a shorter time, or to turn it off altogether. Similarly, most people play games with the backlight on. If you're worried about your charge, you'll probably want to control your games addiction (or, if you really like games, pick up a portable gaming system; the iPod's games are simple, if enduring).

UNDERSTAND THE EQUALIZER

All things being equalized will drain your battery faster. If you like the way the equalizer enhances bass and/or treble, that's fine, but you should know that it requires processing power, and that requires power from the battery.

COMPRESSED IS BEST

Because compression vastly reduces the size of a song file, the iPod can fit more music onto its RAM memory, meaning that the hard drive spins less frequently. Thus, while a sparklingly clear WAV or AIFF file might offer the topmost listening quality, it also delivers the topmost drain on your system. If you must have the highest quality, at least use Apple Lossless (see Chapter 2).

KEEP IT COOL

The battery doesn't like extreme temperatures. For best life, keep your iPod away from direct sunlight and out of cars parked in the sun. Because charging can generate heat, when you're filling it up make sure that your iPod is not wrapped in anything insulating, such as its case. Likewise, it doesn't like very cold temperatures, so don't leave it out to freeze overnight or hide it from your little brother in the refrigerator (the screen is the first thing to go in extreme cold, and those are expensive to replace).

STAY CHARGED, STAY FIT, BUT DON'T OVERDO IT

If you use your iPod infrequently, Apple recommends charging at least every 14 to 18 days. Like your own muscles, if you don't use the battery, it can atrophy. But just to make it more confusing, it turns out that a battery kept at full charge degrades faster, so the ideal is around half-charged. Good luck managing that.

As you can see, there are lots of issues involved with battery life. To reassure you, keep in mind that Apple will replace any battery for $99, and there are kits that let you do it yourself for much less than that. As with so many of the other things people obsess over, it's best to learn enough, then take a deep breath and get on with enjoying yourself. The iPod is supposed to be convenient, liberating you from your stereo, filling your life with song—not a source of stress about keeping your battery *just so*.

How To...

Chapter 4
Taking Control of iTunes

Like many Apple creations, iTunes is deceptively simple. You can fire up the program and use it from day one without being compelled to study in any depth. That's wonderful, except for one thing: while not having to learn obscure commands can free your time, some deeper secrets beneath the smooth gray exterior are powerful tools that can enliven your listening habits, as well as ease the chores of managing your music collection. In fact, if you don't learn these things you're probably missing out on the full iTunes experience.

Of course, iTunes has different abilities to suit different purposes. Some features don't really make sense for people who just need a way to load music onto their Shuffle. Still, learning the ins and outs of iTunes is pretty addictive.

Sort Your Library

Navigating your way through a growing collection of digital music can be initially disorienting, but with a little knowledge about sorting, the shock goes away soon. The longer-term problem is that without the benefit of a physical object like a CD case, it can be easy to forget the contents of your library—all those songs that you've spent so much time collecting fade all too quickly from your mind, and you can't play what you can't remember. Thankfully iTunes is ready to help, offering plenty of ways to scrutinize your songs, so you can recognize—and utilize—all that great stuff.

iTunes helps primarily by giving you the ability to sort everything you've got using a flexible group of categories. It sounds simple, but in practice it's very important. Among its various competitors, iTunes' sorting abilities give it a distinct advantage.

Take a look at the center of the iTunes screen and you'll see that most of its real estate is devoted to sorting and displaying lists of songs, providing several different ways of looking at musical and technical facts (Figure 4-1). Along with the musical data, each song in iTunes contains a bevy of other information stored with it; things like title, artist, genre, and often a whole lot more. We'll talk about ways of editing that data later in this chapter. For now, let's look at the ways to sort the data that's put in your songs by default when you encode (rip) them using iTunes.

Sort by Search

1. Start iTunes.

2. In the **Source** pane on the left, **Library** should be selected. If not, pick it.

3. Enter your search term in the search field, as shown here.

4. As you type, the selection of songs in the main pane decreases dynamically until it finally zeroes in on your search result.

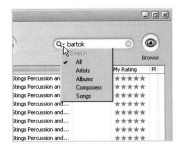

Figure 4-1: *By far the greatest amount of screen space is given over to sorting and displaying songs.*

5. Click at the top of any field to sort the songs beneath. Clicking **Album**, for instance, will group all albums together (shown next) and sort them alphabetically. Click again to switch from descending to ascending order, or vice versa.

6. Double-click a song to play it, or drag and drop it to add it to a playlist at the left (more about playlists in a moment).

7. To clear your search, you can either backspace until the search field is cleared, or click the **X** icon next to your search term.

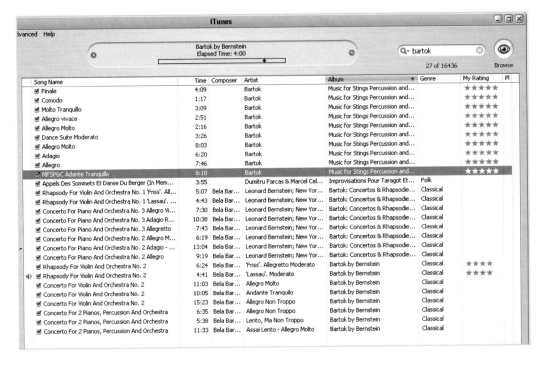

Search works very well for quickly cutting through even the biggest libraries. It can also be a fun way of seeing what you've got. You can try searching on keywords that appear frequently in certain types of songs, as a way of building themed playlists. Search under "baby," "tears," or "time" in any large-ish library and you'll have an instant playlist of mood music.

Browse in iTunes

Other times you might want to sort another way, by quickly scanning what you've got and then drilling down. This is how browsing works in iTunes.

1. Start iTunes.

2. Make sure **Library** is chosen in the **Source** pane.

3. Click the **Browse** icon (a big colorful eye) in the upper right.

TIP

Right-click any of the column headers to choose which column headers are displayed.

---

4. A panel of three columns will descend and push the song listings down the screen. These columns are **Genre**, **Artist**, and **Album**. In their default state, with **All** chosen at the top of each three, your complete library will be displayed below.

5. Scroll through any list to see a genre, artist, or album that appeals to you. When you click an entry, all subsequent columns will be a subset of whatever you've clicked. For instance, if under the **Genre** column you click **Jazz**, only artists with jazz songs will appear in the next column, and only their albums and songs will be shown after that.

6. Skip straight to the part of the iTunes Library you want to get to by clicking the appropriate column header (**Song**, **Artist**, etc.) and then typing the first two or more letters of the thing you're looking for. The iTunes cursor will skip right to that part of the alphabet.

7. Hold the CTRL key (in Windows) or the **Apple** key (on a Mac) while clicking songs, artists, albums, or genres in order to pick and choose several from a list. Hold the SHIFT key to select a whole swath at one time.

8. Click any song to play, or drag and drop to add it to a playlist (more on playlists in a moment).

Create Playlists

While you can certainly scroll merrily through the library on your iPod or in iTunes and randomly pick songs to hear one by one, by far the most practical way to play music is from playlists. The playlist offers several benefits: you can make decisions and then move on to other things, or you can also obsess for hours over creating just the right group of songs to rock the party or pitch your woo. For your iPod, playlists allow it to manage hard drive usage, saving precious energy and adding to its battery life.

Playlists in iTunes come in two basic types, standard and smart. Standard is a simple collection of songs that never changes unless you add or delete something (Figure 4-2). Smart playlists are generated dynamically from a set of criteria and can even be set to update themselves as your library grows. In iTunes you can also save on-the-go playlists that you've created on your iPod and preserve them for posterity (or at least your next trip across town).

File Edit Controls Visualizer Advanced Help

iTunes

Search   Burn Disc

Source	Name	Time	Artist	Album	Genre	My Rating
⚙ Ethiopiques	☑ Let's twist again	2:24	Chubby Checker		Progressive Rock	
⚙ My Top Rated	☑ Lloyd Clark / Japanese Girl	2:31	Various Artists	Scandal Ska	Reggae	
⚙ Psychedelic Rock	☑ Young Blood	2:23	The Coasters	The Coasters		
⚙ Recently Played	☑ 70's disco - Gett Off	3:37	Gett Off	Gett Off	Disco	
⚙ Top 25 Most Played	☑ Push in the Bush	2:47	Push in the Bush	Push in the Bush	Disco	
⚙ Zeppelin's Best	☑ Push It	4:34	Salt N' Peppa	DJ Tools 7	Hip-Hop	
♪ fun	☑ TU-Pac and Dr. Dre	4:45	California Love		Hip-Hop	★★★
♪ funky good list	☑ Hey Ladies (remix)	6:05	Beastie Boys		Hip-Hop	
♪ radio streams	☑ Mr. Big Stuff	2:44	Jean Knight	The Stax Soul Collection	R&B	★★★
♪ rainy day playlist	☑ White Boys	2:28	HAIR	Original Broadway Cast Recording		
♪ summertime	☑ Mega Mix	3:28	Mega Mix	Dhol Blasters		★★★
	☑ Haisai Ojisan (Hey Man!)	3:44	Shoukichi Kina	Asia Classics 2: Peppermint Tea House	World	★★★
	☑ Land Of A Million Drums	4:13	Outkast	Land Of A Million Drums-Promo	Rap	★★★
Selected Song	☑ yurayura teikoku de kangae chu	3:11	yurayura teikoku	Single-01	Rock & Roll	
	☑ Whole Lotta Lovin'	1:40	Fats Domino	Loud, Fast & Out of Control: The Wild Sou...	Rock/Pop	
	☑ Jockamo AKA Iko-Iko - Larry ...	1:33	Various Artists - Fantas...	Creole Kings Of New Orleans		
	☑ Freeze - Albert Collins	2:11	Various Artists - Fuel 2...	T For Texas Blues Masters Volume 1	Blues	★★★
Nothing	☑ Put It On Me	3:56	Lee Fields	Let's Get A Groove On	Soul / Funk / R...	
Selected	☑ Gettin' Funky 'Round Here - Bl...	2:44	Various Artists - Fantas...	The Complete Stax/Volt Soul Singles Volu...		
	☑ Do The Funky Chicken	3:16	Rufus Thomas	The Stax Soul Collection	R&B	

20 songs, 1 hour, 69 MB

Figure 4-2: **A standard playlist with about an hour-and-a-half of dance music**

Create a Standard Playlist

1. Start iTunes.

2. Click **File | New Playlist** (or **Apple**/CTRL-N, or click the **+** icon at the bottom of the **Source** pane). The new list, not yet named, will appear at the bottom of the **Source** pane.

3. Name your new playlist.

4. Click **Library** in the **Source** pane.

5. Drag and drop songs from the library to your new list. To choose more than one song at a time, depress and hold the CTRL key while you pick songs.

6. Click back into your list in the **Source** pane. This will show you the contents of your playlist, in the order of play.

7. Songs can be moved around in any order to suit your preferences. (But you'll want to make sure that the list is sorted by track number; otherwise you won't be able to see your ordering work.)

8. If you're making a list to play for others, now's a good time to try listening to the songs in order and see how they flow together.

Create a Smart Playlist

1. Start iTunes.

2. Click **File | New Smart Playlist**.

3. A dialog box appears. If you'd like to add conditions for your playlist, keep **Match All Of The Following Conditions** checked and use the drop-down menus to set your preferences for this list. For instance, you can choose **Artist**, **Contains**, **Led Zeppelin** to make a playlist of all Zeppelin songs.

4. You can add additional lines of preferences by clicking the + button (or delete a line by clicking the – button next to it). To keep the Zeppelin thing going, you might add another line with **Artist**, **Contains**, **Page Plant**, to logically grow the list. Or you could add **My Rating**, **Is Greater Than**, **[Three Stars]** so that only your top songs by the band would be selected. If you add more than one line of conditions, the first **Match The Following Conditions** checkbox can be set to any or all of the conditions.

5. The next line lets you give the playlist some direction about how it should pick those songs that fit the choices you've just made, as well as tell it how big the list should be. For example, you can decide that it should choose **2 Hours, Selected By Least Recently Played**. That will keep the songs you listen to fresh.

6. If you've unchecked any songs in your library earlier, Smart Playlists includes a field, **Match Only Checked Songs**, that lets you exclude them by only including checked songs.

7. Live Updating keeps track of songs that you've played on your iPod and then pulls them from the playlist; it also adds songs automatically to your playlist if anything

TIP

If you want a playlist made up of full albums grouped together (good for symphonies or concept albums) you can check **Shuffle By Album** in the **Advanced** tab under **Preferences**.

matching its settings is added to your collection. Check **Live Updating** if you'd like that feature. If you want an unchanging list, don't check it.

8. Click **OK**.

9. A playlist will appear in the **Source** pane, automatically named with one of your settings, if appropriate. Our example was called "Led Zeppelin" by default, but we changed it to "Zeppelin's Best" (Figure 4-3).

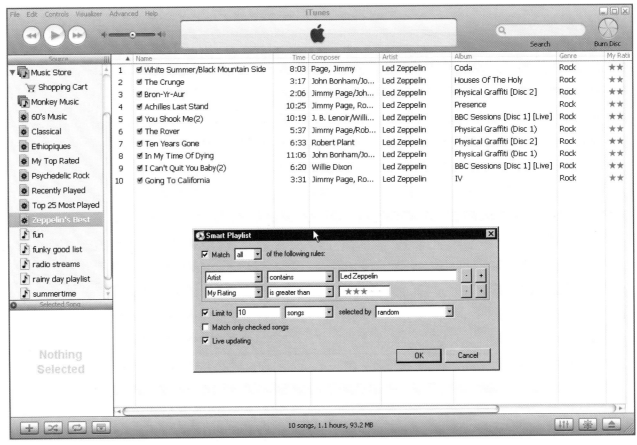

Figure 4-3: A smart playlist can be set with any number of logical categories so you can get just the list you want.

SAVING AN ON-THE-GO PLAYLIST IN iTUNES

We love the On-the-Go playlist feature in the iPod for the way it lets you be spontaneous with playlist creation. You can save an On-the-Go playlist for later, in order to listen to it in iTunes whenever you want. In addition, saving your On-the-Go playlists using this technique means you can have your old On-the-Go playlists on your iPod and still be able to create a new one. Here's how you save an On-the-Go playlist to iTunes.

1. Create an On-the-Go playlist by following the directions in Chapter 3.

2. Connect your iPod to your computer.

3. In iTunes, check out the **Source** pane. You should see **On-the-Go 1 Playlist** listed among your other

Continued . . .

Rate Songs

There are several ways to rate songs in iTunes and on your iPod, and there are several reasons to rate them, including that they help you create Smart Playlists and call up your favorite (or least favorite) songs quickly. The steps that follow show you how to rate songs in the easiest way: right in the iTunes song list.

1. Maximize the iTunes window on your desktop by clicking the box symbol in the upper-right corner. If you can't see the **My Rating** column even with the window maximized, scroll to the right until you can.

2. Click a song. You'll see the section under the **My Rating** column show five little dots (Figure 4-4).

3. Rate the song on a scale of one to five stars by clicking one of the five dots (Figure 4-5). Change your rating by clicking a little to the left or right (you can always change a song's rating).

Figure 4-4: An unrated song in iTunes

SAVING AN ON-THE-GO PLAYLIST IN iTUNES

(Continued)

playlists. If you don't care what your On-the-Go playlists are called, skip to step 7. If you want to change the name as you save the On-the-Go playlist, click it once. (Here's why it's a good idea to name your list: If you chose not to rename the playlist, your next playlist will be called On-the-Go 2, the next one On-the-Go 3, and so on. Whether you go the automatic or manual naming route, these playlists will live on in your iPod and in iTunes until you delete them using iTunes.)

4. Wait a couple of seconds.

5. Click it again to highlight it for editing.

6. Change the name of the playlist.

7. That's it—you're done.

8. To create another On-the-Go playlist, disconnect your iPod and be on your way. You can create an On-the-Go playlist in exactly the same way you did before because every time you sync your iPod with iTunes, the list gets saved as an actual, non-On-the-Go playlist, as just described, leaving the space for on-the-go lists clear and ready for more.

☑ Amethyst Nightgown	2:49	Sun City Girls	Box Of Chameleons (Disc 2)	Rock
☑ A Random Finale	2:25	Sun City Girls	Box Of Chameleons (Disc 2)	Rock ★★★★
☑ Plecostamus	2:08	Sun City Girls	Box Of Chameleons (Disc 2)	Rock
☑ Toba Hightop	2:19	Sun City Girls	Box Of Chameleons (Disc 2)	Rock
☑ Lifting The Hemline Of The Unknown	2:21	Sun City Girls	Box Of Chameleons (Disc 2)	Rock
☑ A Photogenic Memory	0:59	Sun City Girls	Box Of Chameleons (Disc 2)	Rock
☑ Bobby Sands	1:30	Sun City Girls	Box Of Chameleons (Disc 2)	Rock
☑ The Eleven, Oh Nine In The Refrigerator, ...	1:55	Sun City Girls	Box Of Chameleons (Disc 2)	Rock
☑ The Crowbar Of Illusion	2:52	Sun City Girls	Box Of Chameleons (Disc 2)	Rock
☑ The Big Purr	1:02	Sun City Girls	Box Of Chameleons (Disc 2)	Rock
☑ A Throne's Stow	0:19	Sun City Girls	Box Of Chameleons (Disc 2)	Rock

Figure 4-5: Now the song's rated.

Figure 4-6: The right-click method's quick and easy.

This technique works great for rating a lot of songs because you can just skip right down the song list. Another of the several ways you can rate songs is by right-clicking a song and choosing **My Rating** from the pop-up menu (Figure 4-6). It's worth checking out what else is in that menu; there's some really useful stuff.

FIXING iTUNES IF IT STARTS STUTTERING

Every once in a while—especially after installing new audio hardware or software on a Windows computer—you might notice iTunes stutter during playback. You'll hear a fast skipping, repeated maybe two or three times per second, with silence in between each skip. It's not subtle; you'll recognize it clearly. Here's how to fix that.

1. Close iTunes.

2. Go to **Start** menu | **Control Panel**, or follow whatever steps you normally take to open the Windows Control Panel.

3. Double-click the **QuickTime** menu item.

4. Go to **SoundOut** in the drop-down menu at the top (there are a lot of items there; **SoundOut** is about two-thirds of the way down).

5. In the **Choose A Device For Playback** drop-down menu, choose **waveOut** instead of **DirectSound**.

6. Close the **QuickTime Settings** window.

Song Information: Actually a Big Deal

You could use iTunes for years and never know what an ID3 tag was, even though you'd been using them all along. ID3 tags are the part of your MP3 files that contains the song information: song title, album, artist, and a bunch of other stuff. Just about any digital music file type uses ID3 tags, from AAC to . . . well, there aren't any that end with Z. But you get the point.

iTunes calls this song information Song Info, and it's what allows your iPod to categorize music by artist, album, composer, and so on. These tags can tell you a lot about your files—and when they don't, you can add the information yourself.

Edit Song Information

If you ripped CDs while your computer wasn't connected to the Internet, you have a bunch of songs called "Track 1"—not much help when it comes to finding the music you're looking for in iTunes or on your iPod. You may also have ripped CDs in other programs that use other naming conventions, so each song will have a track number at the beginning of the file name (in the worst-case scenario, the song will be called "01 Track 1"). Or maybe you download songs from file-sharing networks and have songs encoded by people all over the world in every which way, often without proper song information.

Here's how you can edit the song information for any track in iTunes.

1. Right-click any song in the iTunes song list—ideally one that has an incorrect or incomplete information for song title, album, or artist (Figure 4-7). Choose **Get Info** from the pop-up menu.

2. Click on the **Info** tab. Once there you can fill out as much as you want (Figure 4-8). The general rule is that you should at least fill out the **Name**, **Artist**, and **Album** fields. The more you fill out, the more ways you'll be able to classify your music library later and make it easier to track stuff down, especially when you're trying to build a Smart Playlist of songs that fit specific criteria.

Figure 4-7: *This song has no artist listed.*

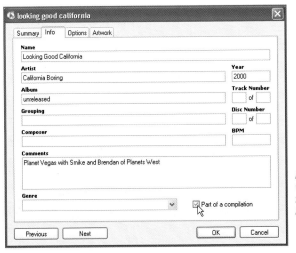

Figure 4-8: *We capitalized the words in the song title and filled out most of the rest of the information.*

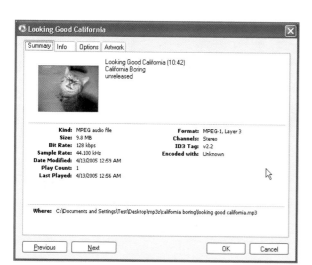

Figure 4-9: *The Summary tab knows all. Well, almost. OK . . . some.*

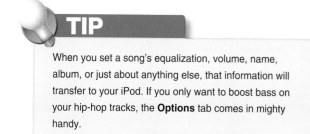

TIP

When you set a song's equalization, volume, name, album, or just about anything else, that information will transfer to your iPod. If you only want to boost bass on your hip-hop tracks, the **Options** tab comes in mighty handy.

3. The **Summary** tab tells you the technical details about a song. In Figure 4-9, the **Kind** (MPEG audio file) and **Format** (MPEG-1, Layer 3) mean that it's an MP3 file. The other fields tell us that it was created by an unknown encoder with a 128 Kbps bit rate, in stereo, at the normal sample rate, and that we've only played it once.

4. In the **Options** tab (Figure 4-10), you can set a song to always play at a certain volume, set the equalizer, and change the rating. You could also set a song to only play from a certain point to another point, but we've found scarce use for that.

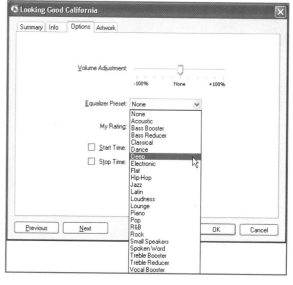

Figure 4-10: *You can meddle with a song's volume and equalization at your leisure.*

5. Finally, in the **Artwork** tab (Figure 4-11), you can change album art. This is especially important with the iPod Photo, since the image you choose here is what shows up when the song plays.

6. Click the **Next** or **Previous** button to change the song information for other tracks in your library, or click **OK** if you're done altering the song information.

EDITING MULTIPLE SONGS' INFORMATION

You can edit the song information for a whole slew of songs at the same time, changing just about everything (except artwork) for all of them in one fell swoop—a real timesaver.

1. Sort the iTunes Library in such a way that it puts a bunch of songs whose information you want to change right next to each other. (See the tips on sorting songs later on in this chapter.)

2. Hold down the SHIFT key and use the arrow keys or mouse to select multiple songs. You can also peck around for certain songs by holding down the CTRL key.

3. Once you have everything selected that you want to modify, right-click any of the selected items. Choose **Get Info** from the dialog box that appears.

4. The **Multiple Song Information** screen will open, containing many of the elements we altered in the "Edit Song Information" section, except there will be places for checkmarks next to the fields. Just fill in the information you want to apply to all of the selected songs, and then click OK. Remember that any change you make here will affect all songs.

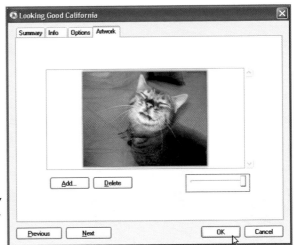

Figure 4-11: "Crush" clearly loves this song.

Tweak Your Experience

In this section, you'll tweak audio and visual settings to enhance your listening experience.

Set Audio Preferences

Tired of straining to hear some songs while being startled by the volume of others? Want a smooth segue from song to song? iTunes offers several experience-enhancing features, accessed under **Preferences**, that can smooth some rough audio edges (Figure 4-12).

DJs use crossfading to smoothly transition from song to song, so that before one song has fully ended the next one slowly fades in. iTunes has an automated crossfading system that can be set to deliver from 0 to 12 seconds of overlap between songs.

Sound Enhancer is a one-stop, foolproof utility that does exactly what its name implies by giving bass and treble a little boost and enhancing stereo separation. Try it out and see if you like it, as opinions are mixed.

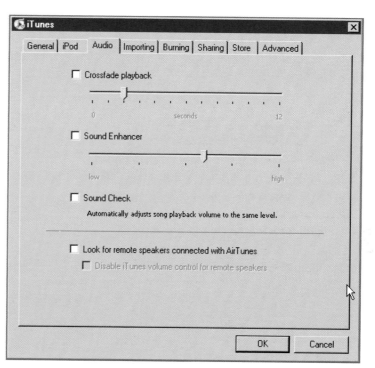

Figure 4-12: Audio preferences can enhance your listening experience and smooth the rough edges.

iTune's utility for stabilizing playback volume is called Sound Check. When Sound Check is on, iTunes analyzes all the songs for volume and notes what it finds. On playback, it uses this information to raise or lower playback volume to keep things at an even keel.

1. Open **Edit** I **Preferences**. Click the **Audio** tab.

2. **Crossfade Playback** is set by default. If you don't like it, turn it off. If you like it, use the slider to tweak the length of the transitions from song to song.

3. Click **Sound Enhancer** and listen to how it sounds. You might like it—or not. Some people prefer other options, such as EQ (described later).

4. If you want to use **Sound Check**, click it. If your library is large, iTunes will spend a lot of time checking each track and assigning a volume rating to it. This might slow your computer for a time, but it won't permanently change the sound of any of your files, and it only needs to check each song once.

5. The final checkbox is to enable AirTunes-compatible speakers, which use Apple's system for in-home networking. Click this box if you have them set up and want iTunes to use them; read Chapter 8 for more information about home networks.

6. All changes are instantly implemented so you can test them out while the dialog box is still open.

7. When you're satisfied with your adjustments, click **OK**.

The Visualizer

If iTunes had been around in the '60s, a lot more hippies would have stayed home. Whether that's a good thing or not, at least one of us is oddly addicted to listening to his spaciest music with this swirly, pulsing lightshow uncannily throbbing with the tunes. It's fun, nonpretentious abstract art in the tradition of fireworks and the laser light show.

For those of you who have also caught this bug, we offer the tools to give your slack-jawed gazing some spine: Table 4-1 lists the commands that let you take control of the Visualizer for yourself.

The patterns of the Visualizer are made of three basic parameters: wave forms, visual effects, and colors. Change these and you change the picture in ways that are sometimes subtle, sometimes stunning. Altering the picture is done essentially by cycling through the many presets in each category to combine them in different ways. (The names of the presets—"waterfall of life," "angel's caress," and "tripping hard"—certainly seem like they were named at a vintage Grateful Dead show.)

Set Visualizer Presets

Frame rate is determined by your computer's processing power and the size of the display: the stronger your computer, the faster your frame rate and the smoother the animations. If you have a computer with a slow processor, you

COMMAND	WHAT IT DOES	DETAILS
H or ?	Displays **Help** menu.	Some, but not all, of these commands are documented in the **Help** menu.
I	Displays track info.	Title, artist, and album are displayed.
LEFT and RIGHT ARROWS	Skips to the next song in either direction.	Lets you move through the tunes without breaking the visual spell.
UP and DOWN ARROWS	Raises or lowers the volume.	Lets you change the volume without stopping the Visualizer.
C	Displays current settings.	Shows which three presets are currently running.
M	Switches "mode."	Lets you pick whether patterns are displayed with random parameters, those set by the user, or frozen and unchanging. Pick **Freeze** when you're setting the parameters so the screen doesn't change on you.
Q/W	Toggles wave form.	Changes the shape of the lines that move to the music like an old radio oscillator.
A/S	Toggles visual effect.	Cycles through all of the different visual effects.
Z/X	Toggles color.	Changes the color scheme.
SHIFT-0 TO SHIFT-9	Saves current pattern.	Assigns the current pattern to a number, for later recall.
0 to 9	Plays assigned pattern.	Plays back the patterns that you've saved with the previous command.
D	Clears assigned patterns.	Erases any patterns you've stored.
N	Toggles high or low contrast colors.	Displays better on some monitors. See which you prefer.
T	Toggles the frame rate cap.	Caps the frame rate at 30 frames per second, which is fast enough for smoothly animated effects.

Table 4-1: Take Control of the Visualizer

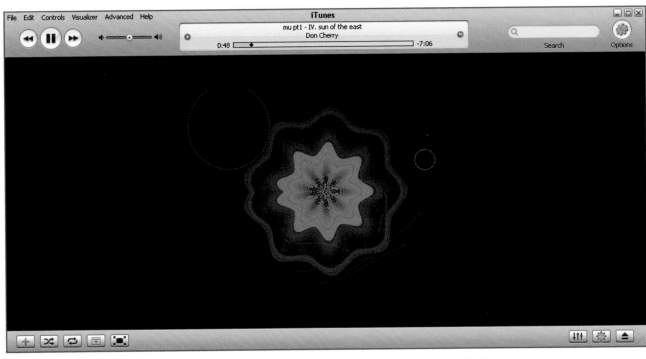

Figure 4-13: Visualizer is a hypnotic random visual display that moves and changes in time with the music.

might want to stick with small or medium size. Experiment and see what works best. On the other hand, if your processor is very fast, things could get out of hand. If so, toggle the frame rate.

1. Play a song, or better yet, begin a playlist.

2. Open the **Visualizer** menu and select the size of display you want: **Small**, **Medium**, **Large**, or **Full-Screen**.

3. Click **Visualizer | Turn Visualizer On** (or CTRL-T).

4. Click M to freeze.

If nothing seems to happen at first, don't freak out, dude! For most of the changes you'll want to wait at least six seconds. Soon you'll be seeing stars (Figure 4-13).

CAUTION

It's a good idea to leave your computer alone during the burning process, to avoid any drain in processing power that could cause an error writing your disc. Similarly, you probably want to turn off any screen savers, especially those that are processor-intensive.

UICKSTEPS

BURNING DISCS

1. Before you burn your disc, set your preferences. Click **Edit | Preferences** and then click the **Burning** tab in the dialog box. This will list your CD burner if it was correctly detected by iTunes. Choose the preferred speed for burning—**Maximum Possible** is usually best. Choose your **Disc Format**.

2. If you choose **Audio CD**, iTunes lets you pick how much time you want between songs (two seconds is the default and you'll probably want to stick pretty close to this).

3. Choose a playlist that you want to burn. If you're burning an audio CD, make sure the total time is less than 70 minutes, or you'll have to split your song over two or more discs.

4. Check **Use Sound Check** if you'd like to keep the sound level of all songs relatively equal. This will prevent any nerve-wracking jumps in volume. Close **Preferences**.

Continued . . .

If there's one thing that mars the Visualizer experience it is the intermittent appearance of the Apple logo, which looks almost cult-like when your eyes are glazed over from staring at the patterns and colors. At the beginning is fine, but when you're really into your music this exercise in branding is pretty invasive.

Burn CDs

Maybe you really like the playlist you made for your road trip last year, and now you want to send it to your sister for her cross-country drive? Or you love the songs you bought on iTunes but want to play them in your car CD player? You're in luck! iTunes comes packed with the capability to burn CDs—provided, of course, that your computer is equipped with a CD burner.

iTunes uses the playlist as its main interface for CD burning. You'll notice that whenever you click a list, the big icon in the top right of iTunes changes to the **Burn Disc** option—a good example of efficient design. iTunes doesn't need another interface for making lists of tracks to burn.

The main choice you need to make, aside from what to put on your CD, is whether it will be an MP3 CD, data CD, or audio CD. Audio CDs play in all standard CD players, and some CD players can handle MP3s these days, but so far few can play AAC files. If you have a list of AAC files and choose MP3 as the disc type, iTunes will convert those songs. The big advantage of MP3 and data CDs is that they will hold a lot more songs than a standard audio CD because they're compressed.

Manage Your Music Library

Now that you oversee a growing iTunes Library, you'll want to consider your options for organizing it. The essential question is how much power do you want to hand over to iTunes, and conversely, how much time do you want to spend keeping track of files? Do you want your music all in one folder? Or would you prefer to keep some files separate for other purposes? Under

BURNING DISCS

(*Continued*)

5. Click the **Burn Disc** icon in the top right. It will quickly morph into an eerie, radioactive warning. (Why? Who knows?)

6. iTunes will ask you to insert a blank disc. Do it.

7. If the disc is acceptably blank, iTunes will ask you to click **Burn Disc** once again to begin burning. When you do, the radioactive sign will begin to pulsate. It looks dangerous, but it's not.

8. iTunes will now begin writing to disc. You can watch the progress in the main pane.

9. Once your disc is written it will pop out on its tray. If you're burning more than one, iTunes will ask you to insert another CD.

Preferences | **Advanced**, you can check **Keep iTunes Music Folder Organized**, which will enable iTunes to put your music imported from non-iTunes sources into folders based on artist and album and rename the files based on their tagged information.

This is basically like hiring a maid to straighten up your mess: it may not be exactly how you would do it yourself, but at least it's organized. iTunes does this organization by making copies of songs in your library. The downside to this is that you'll have two copies of anything that you didn't rip in iTunes, so you're still looking at some cleanup after tidying is done.

Basic Issues of iTunes Organization

Most of the library management tools are under the **Advanced** tab in **Preferences** (Figure 4-14). You can confirm your folder location.

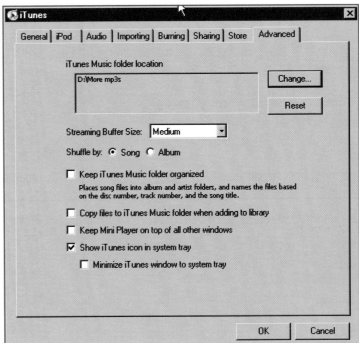

Figure 4-14: The Advanced tab under Preferences contains some suitably advanced options for organizing your music.

QUICKSTEPS

SETTING PODCAST PREFERENCES

1. Click **Edit | Preferences**. The iTunes dialog box will open.

2. Click the **Podcasts** tab.

3. Choose how often you want iTunes to check for new episodes from the dropdown list. Set a frequency that matches your listening habits.

4. Choose what you want iTunes to do when it finds new episodes. You'll probably want to select **Download Most Recent One**, since that's why you've subscribed.

5. Finally, decide if you want to keep old episodes, and if so how far back. iTunes lets you keep as many as 10 previous episodes, or all of them. Balance how likely you are to listen to these old episodes against how much spare disk space you've got.

6. Click **OK** when you're finished.

The next item is **Streaming Buffer Size,** used when you are streaming sounds from over the Internet, something we'll look at in Chapter 9.

Shuffle by Song/Album lets you decide if you want whole albums played all the way through, or just songs, when your music shuffles.

Keep iTunes Music Folder Organized looks mild enough, but when you check it, your music files will be copied and put into folders of iTunes' choosing, based, as it says, "on the disc number, track number, and the song title." As mentioned, this can be very handy, but you must track down the originals and decide what to do with them.

Copy Files To iTunes Music Folder is very similar to the previous option: if you check this option, whenever you add a file to the library (essentially just making iTunes aware of the song and its location), iTunes will also copy that song and put it into your iTunes folder.

One of the best reasons for using all of these file management features is if you're using a computer in a place where you might have to leave with little notice. For instance, you might get a new computer at work (or you might be asked to leave yourself). Knowing that your collection is all filed in one place can make the change much easier.

Configure Podcast Updates

Do you take your iPod with you everyday to listen to your favorite programs of podcasts on your way to work? Or do you only listen to podcasts every month or so when you take the train to visit your folks? No matter the frequency, you may want to update your iTunes settings to match your schedule (Figure 4-15).

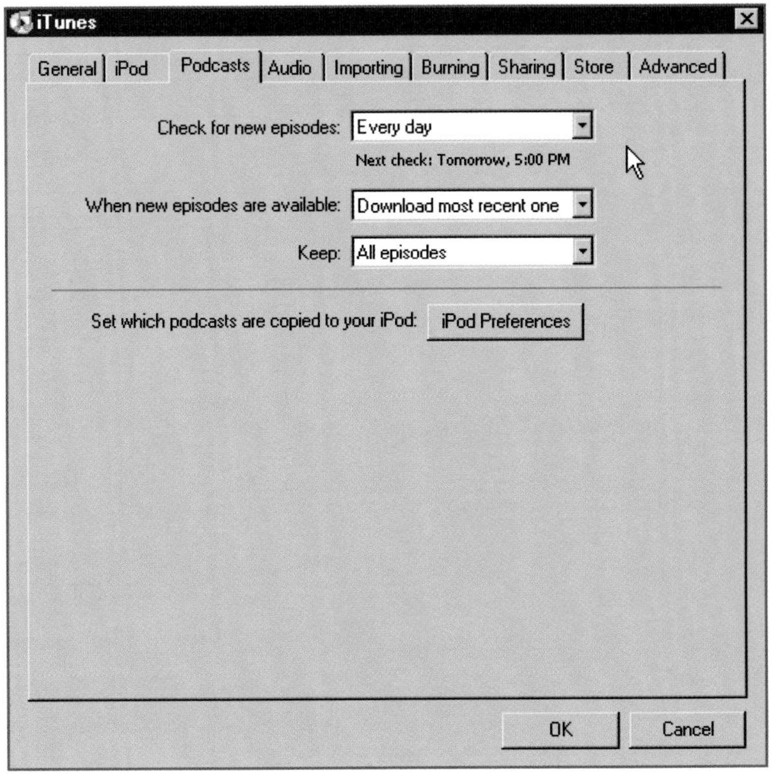

Figure 4-15: Podcasting preferences let you sync iTunes' podcasting activities with your listening schedule.

Podcast preferences will let you tweak things like how often iTunes checks for new episodes of your podcasts; which programs are copied to your iPod; and whether to store or trash old episodes. Handy stuff for good hygiene with your iPod and iTunes.

Chapter 5

Getting the Best Sound Quality

Since you've spent a lot of time ripping your CDs or buying songs at the iTunes store, it would be a shame if you didn't take full advantage of them. But that's just what you're doing if your sound quality isn't good. Of course, there's no getting around the fact that with the iPod you're listening to music on a portable device and it's not going to match a high-end audio system. But the sound of the iPod can be remarkably great, especially if you spend a little effort getting it right.

In fact, most of the audio snobs we know who used to sniff at the low quality of MP3 sound are surprised when we demonstrate just what kind of sound is possible by adding a good set of headphones or hooking up those little players to some decent speakers. And even if they weren't impressed, *we* are, and personal pleasure is what it's all about.

Make Your Music Sound Good

This chapter will go over some important tweaks that can enhance your sound dramatically, on both your iPod and your computer running iTunes. By adding a good set of headphones, making sure you've got a good sound card installed on your home computer, and perhaps adding an iTunes audio plug-in, you can give your listening experience a new boost and get the most out of your musical investment.

Digital technology doesn't require prototyping, shipping, and all the other expenses real-world devices require. That means iTunes, with its solid dedication to good sound, is a great platform for adding features that developers dream up. We'll review a couple of good choices next. As the iPod and iTunes revolution rolls on, you can expect to see more and more interesting audio enhancers—at least for iTunes. For the moment, Apple is keeping a close lid on iPod development.

The Overwhelming Importance of Headphones

This chapter is dedicated to sound quality, so we'd be remiss if we didn't cover headphones: they're the number one factor in determining how good your iPod sounds. The same goes for the speakers in your home system—it makes sense, if you think about it; turning electricity into sound is a complicated process. Your headphones and speakers definitely affect sound quality more than any other factor.

In stark contrast to MP3 players such as your iPod, headphones have been around for over a century, when their ancestors helped the first telephones turn electricity into sound. Maybe that's why there are so many different types of headphones that use a tremendous variety of technologies to reproduce sound for our ears. Here's how they line up.

CAUTION

Good headphones cost a lot. If you don't have the cash for the high-end models and want to try something other than the earbuds that come with the iPod, you can pick up a decent pair for $30 or so. But if you're serious about sound quality, we recommend saving up and springing for something in at least the $100 range.

The Included Earbuds

We wouldn't expect Apple to include high-end headphones with every iPod—the economics wouldn't make sense—and many people are perfectly happy with the earbuds that Apple does provide. They sound better than the headphones included with most other MP3 players, and their white wire lets the world know you're packing an iPod. However, if the included earbuds don't fit your ear properly, or if you'd like to explore better-sounding models with various designs, read on.

Apple In-Ear Headphones

Apple sells these as an accessory for $39. They're a big improvement over the earbuds that come with the iPod, and many people prefer the way their rubber forms a seal with the ear canal, keeping noise out and bass in. Plus, they let you keep the white wire look. However, headphone experts we know say it's generally worth paying more for someone else's in-ear headphones, if you want high-end sound.

Over-the-Ear Headphones

Otherwise known as *circumaural* headphones, these cover your entire ear, in some cases without touching the ear itself. Sizes and specs vary considerably, but they come in two basic types: closed-back and open-back. Your choice depends on where you want to use your headphones, the type of music you're listening to, and your own sonic predilections.

CLOSED-BACK

Closed-back headphones form a seal around the entire ear and trap the sound in the little chamber they form against your ear (Figure 5-1). The closed-back design blocks outside noise without making you resort to high volumes. AKG, Beyerdynamic, Bose, Grado, Koss, Sennheiser, and Sony all make very good over-the-ear headphones.

QUICK**FACTS**

COMPARING SOUND ISOLATION WITH NOISE CANCELLATION

There are two ways to prevent outside noise from competing with the music in your headphones: by using sound isolation or by using active noise cancellation.

Sound isolation means you block the sound physically by forming a seal around the ear or with the ear canal.

Active noise cancellation, on the other hand, samples outside noise with little microphones on the headphone, inverts that signal, and mixes it with your audio in real time, which effectively cancels out the noise of jet engines, motors, and other persistent sources. If that sounds too technical, think of noise cancellation as an electronic blocker of background noise that you can turn on or off (batteries required).

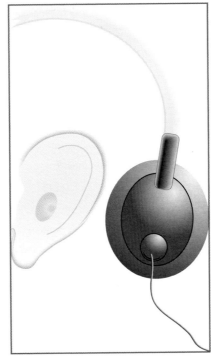

Figure 5-1: *Closed-back over-the-ear headphones help trap sound inside while blocking any outside noise.*

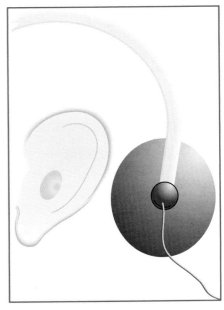

Figure 5-2: *Open-back headphones let sound in and out, which helps retain clarity. They might also earn you some looks from people around you who can hear your tunes.*

TIP

We could fill an entire book with descriptions of the vast array of headphone models out there, and to highlight a few models here wouldn't do them justice. We mention a few brands in this chapter but recommend that you search the Web for headphone reviews and find websites that objectively review headphones (CNET.com, headphone .com, etc.). You can usually find better prices online, but that means waiting a few days before you get the headphones.

OPEN-BACK

Open-back type models still surround your ear (Figure 5-2) but they're open in the back (not literally—they're typically covered by a screen of some kind). Audiophiles, or people who love (and gladly pay for) high-end sound, generally prefer the open-back design for its sonic clarity. The way the closed-back design traps sound can cause sound issues (to the ears of the high-end audio enthusiast, anyway). AKG, Beyerdynamic, Grado, Koss, and Sennheiser make very respectable open-back over-the-ear headphones.

TIP

If your headphones require a lot of power to make sound, they have a high impedance. The iPod puts out 30mW (milliwatts) of power per channel, which is a lot (rumor has it this is due to Steve Jobs' partial deafness). However, if you use your iPod with headphones that were designed for home use and want the very best sound quality, consider buying a portable amplifier; check out our section on portable amplifiers in Chapter 7. (We don't use them ourselves because it means carrying around another piece of gear, and after our iPods, cell phones, and headphones, there's not much more we're willing to carry.)

TIP

Open-back headphones leak a lot of sound, especially at high volumes. If you're often in situations that require a certain degree of silence, go with closed-back. On the other hand, some people like to blast their music on open-back earphones in public, so that everyone knows what they're listening to. You know who you are!

ON-THE-EAR HEADPHONES

These headphones are smaller but also come in open- and closed-back varieties. The pads typically rest on the outside of your ear rather than against your head (Figure 5-3). They're more portable, but they can't reproduce the lower bass frequencies the larger ones can.

Because they're lighter, some on-the-ear headphones come with neck bands that go around the back of your head or ear clips that hold the headphones to your ears. Like so many other headphone-related features, this is a matter of personal preference. Another advantage: they're more portable than full-size over-the-ear headphones and often fold up to fairly small sizes.

AKG, Grado, Sennheiser, and Sony make decent on-the-ear headphones.

In-Ear Headphones

Experts agree that open-back over-the-ear headphones produce the best sound under ideal circumstances, but when do those happen? Our lives are busy, and often spent on the go. In-ear headphones are small enough to coil up and stash just about anywhere, and they can produce sound on par with over-the-ear and on-the-ear models.

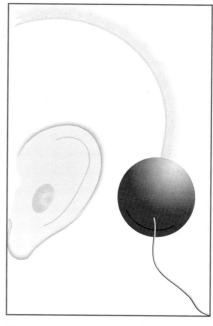

Figure 5-3: The medium-sized on-the-ear headphone style was the default when personal music players first became popular.

EARBUDS (UNSEALED)

You already have earbuds of this type since they came with your iPod, so if you're considering replacing them, you should probably think about another design. But if you like unsealed earbuds for another reason (such as that you have a better chance of hearing traffic with them) and the ones that came with your iPod don't fit your ears, you might consider buying a replacement pair of unsealed earbuds (Figure 5-4).

Figure 5-4:
Unsealed earbuds are the type that comes with the iPod. If you like that style but want a few improvements, do some comparing.

IN-EAR HEADPHONES (SEALED)

The sealed type of in-ear headphone is the critical favorite as far as compact, in-ear headphones go, although when it comes to over-the-ear headphones, those same critics tend to prefer the unsealed variety (Figure 5-5). They pump low bass, high treble, and every sound between straight into your ear canal, and they require a lot less juice to create volume than other models do. When you walk with sealed in-ear headphones, however, the cable can scrape against your clothes and cause all sorts of noise interference due to the headphone's tight

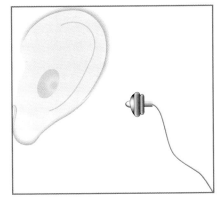

Figure 5-5: In-ear headphones deliver quality sound at lower power levels. Just be careful when you're wearing them in public that you don't completely isolate yourself—that could be dangerous.

seal with your ear canal. To avoid this, you can either route the cable so that it doesn't scrape on anything, or go with a differently designed headphone for active listening.

The best in-ear sealed headphones come from Etymotic, Shure, and Sony.

iTunes Equalization

Just as most stereos have bass and treble controls, iTunes has a similar equalization feature, except it has 10 bands (32 Hz to 16 kHz) instead of a stereo's two bands (plain old bass and treble). You can access it anytime during playback by clicking the small **EQ** button.

Set EQ in iTunes

This is fairly simple, although there are a few things to keep in mind.

1. Once you've clicked the **EQ** button to bring up the **Equalizer** window, click the **On** checkbox at the upper left (Figure 5-6); otherwise, nothing you change will affect anything.

2. Start with a preset by selecting one from the drop-down menu (Figure 5-7). Manual gives you a flat response; you can guess what the others mean. Pick one; if it sounds good on your speakers or headphones, you might be done.

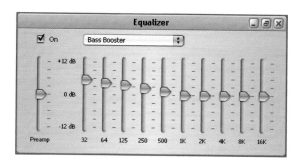

Figure 5-6: **The iTunes Equalizer window is fairly easy to use, once you remember to click the On checkbox.**

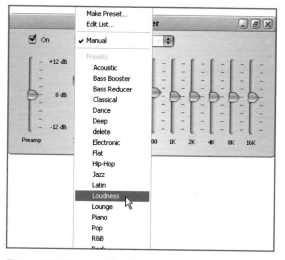

Figure 5-7: **Try a variety of presets to figure out which ones you might like. If your speakers lack bass, for instance, try Bass Booster or Loudness.**

QUICKSTEPS

ATTACHING AN EQ SETTING TO A SONG

Sometimes a song just needs a little something to give it a boost. By using one of the many preset EQ settings, most of which are designed for a particular genre, the sound can be equalized in a way that suits it well.

1. Locate your song in the **center** pane. You've learned to do this a variety of ways.

2. Right-click your song.

3. Choose **Get Info**.

4. When the **Songs** dialog box pops up, choose the **Options** tab.

5. Under **Options**, you are presented with a few choices that affect sound quality. Since you're there for the EQ, select whatever **EQ Preset** you'd like to use.

Remember that this EQ will now stick with your song, so if you get tired of it, you'll have to go back in and use the same procedure to remove it.

TIP

With most shareware, Windows choices are better than those on the Mac side. But if you use a Macintosh, your choices in iTunes plug-ins will be much wider than in the Windows' world.

3. You can fiddle around with the individual bands. This is especially helpful when playing iTunes through speakers, since rooms vary so much in size and sound absorbency. Some rooms kill bass naturally, while others are too bright and cause high frequencies to ring out.

4. Sometimes it helps to toggle the **On** button on and off to check your setting against a flat one, just to see what it's doing.

5. If you create a setting that works for you, make your own EQ preset. To do this, choose the **Make Preset** selection at the top of the drop-down menu (Figure 5-8).

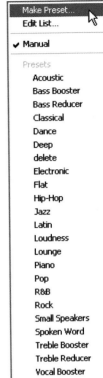

Figure 5-8: After saving a preset, you can call it back with a few clicks, rather than setting the slider on each of the ten bands in the exact same place manually.

Third-Party Sound Enhancers

Speakers and headphones have the biggest impact on how iTunes and your iPod sound. You can affect your sound with iTunes' own equalizer settings or use one of the plug-ins we discuss in this section to make your digital music sound better. Purist audiophiles think CDs sound inferior to vinyl, that it's worth spending over $10,000 on a sound system, and that compressed formats such as AAC, MP3, OGG, and WMA are fairly worthless. (As far as digital formats go, they'd be likely to go with Apple Lossless for use on the iPod and in iTunes). They have traditionally eschewed various EQ and sound enhancers because they believe that they tamper with the producer and engineers' work in mixing the original album down.

That said, from our experience, we can certainly appreciate the difference these third-party plug-ins make with compressed files, and surely audiophiles trying to eke high-quality sound out of mediocre speakers would have to agree.

CAUTION

You can use Octiv Volume Logic for 14 days for free; after that it costs $20. If you decide it's not worth paying for, we recommend uninstalling the program from the **Control Panel**. Otherwise, you'll get a nag screen every time you start iTunes.

CAUTION

If you installed iTunes in a directory other than the default one it picks automatically, you'll need to show the Octiv Volume Logic installer where you installed iTunes.

Whether they make enough difference to be worth the $20–$25 it costs to keep them after the trial period runs out is up to you.

Apple hasn't allowed outside developers to make plug-ins for the iPod, which means you're limited to the presets Apple included with the version of the iPod Updater you ran last. iTunes, on the other hand, can allow downloadable plug-ins to process your sound in ways that it cannot process on its own.

Octiv Volume Logic

Developed by a company called Octiv (now a division of Plantronics), Volume Logic was the first audio plug-in for iTunes. The program is really simple to install and configure. To purchase it, go to http://octiv.com and enter your credit card information. You'll get a serial number, which will activate the program permanently.

Once you've installed Volume Logic, harnessing its powers is a matter of finding the right settings for your ears and speakers or headphones. There are 19 presets to choose from; we recommend choosing **General** (Figure 5-9), but some situations call for other presets (the **Small Speakers** preset is a great example).

Once you've selected a preset, use the two slider controls—Drive and Bass Boost—to exert a little more control over how Octiv Volume Logic affects your sound in iTunes (Figure 5-10).

INSTALL OCTIV VOLUME LOGIC

In order for the Octiv plug-in to install itself properly, iTunes needs to be closed.

1. Close iTunes, either by clicking the **X** in the upper-right corner or going to **File | Exit**.
2. Go to http://www.octiv.com/.
3. Click the **Downloads** link and download the iTunes plug-in for either Mac or Windows, depending on which operating system you use, by clicking the button for **iTunes Mac** or **iTunes PC**.
4. Choose **Run** from the menu that pops up right after you click the button.

RIDING THE SLIDERS

Here's what each **slider control** does in the Octiv
Volume Logic window.

- **Drive**   If you're familiar with audio effects, whether
  through guitar pedals or audio editing, you might
  call this "feedback." It controls how much the effect
  affects the sound by mixing a clean, uneffected
  signal with an Octiv-processed version at variable
  levels.

- **Bass Boost**   This one sounds simple, but aside
  from merely amplifying the bass frequencies,
  Bass Boost adds resonance to other frequencies.
  Everyone has different tastes and different music, so
  again, experimentation is key.

CAUTION

If you use too much Bass Boost with small, subwooferless
speakers, your overall volume will lower because as it
raises lower frequencies, it quiets the higher frequencies
your speakers can put out.

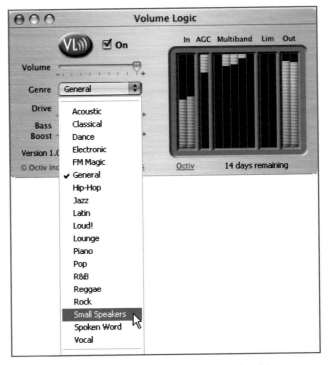

*Figure 5-9: We recommend General, but you should
experiment . . . maybe something else will work better for you.*

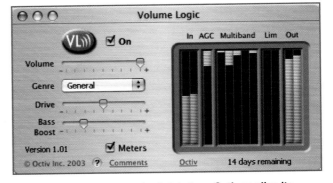

*Figure 5-10: These controls dictate how Octiv applies its
sound enhancement algorithms to your music.*

UNDERSTAND VOLUME LOGIC'S METERS

You can use Volume Logic by picking a preset and maybe tweaking the sliders a few times, but if you really want to know what's going on under the hood, here's what the meters' names mean in plain English.

- **In (Input)**   This shows you how much volume the song has. You can use it to see how good a job iTunes' Sound Check feature is doing (you should see little variation from song to song).

- **AGC (Automatic Gain Control)**   This meter reflects how much work Volume Logic's volume normalizer is doing in order to level out the currently playing song's volume.

- **Multiband**   Here's where the program figures out how much to raise various EQ bands and then recalibrates the equalization of each song. If you have Volume Logic on, iTunes' Equalizer Settings won't do much because Octiv's program adjusts the EQ after iTunes does.

- **Lim (Final Limiter)**   This meter shows how much Volume Logic's limiter function is eliminating any remaining sections that are too loud.

- **Out (Output)**   The plug-in outputs the processed sound at the level indicated by this meter. If the AGC and limiter do their jobs, you'll never see the Output meter fill up completely.

Bloggers can find plenty of plug-ins online that post what they're currently playing to their web page, but this chapter's about enhancing sound, so we'll stick with those types of additions. Octiv's Volume Logic is the most popular option for both Mac and Windows, but Mac users have another option: SubBand.

SubBand (Mac Only)

As this book is being written, the only other audio plug-in for iTunes is a Mac-only program (OS X required) called SubBand, developed by one of the guys who made the Winamp software music player. If you have Mac OS X 10.3 and want to try an alternative to Octiv Volume Logic, perhaps you'll choose SubBand instead. It's shareware and costs $25 to register.

TIP

If you want to get rid of the meters and reduce the size of the **Volume Logic** window, uncheck the **Meters** box. To see what your **Volume Logic** settings are doing to your music, toggle the effect on and off by unchecking the **On** box.

CAUTION

Sometimes when you turn a plug-in on or off, you can trigger a large change in volume. It's never a good idea to change volume settings while your headphones are on your ears. In fact, you should always take your headphones off before you activate a plug-in or hit Play on anything that's connected to your ears, in order to prevent damaging your ears, of which you have only two.

5

Get Cleaner, Truer Sound from Your Computer

Like the other files you have on your computer's hard drive, the music you've been keeping there (and on your iPod) is stored in 1's and 0's. When you play a song on your computer, iTunes applies a decoder algorithm and first sends the audio through your sound driver and finally to your sound card (or in the case of some computers, the part of the motherboard that deals with sound). There, the digital audio gets turned into electricity, which then powers your headphones or outputs to your stereo system. (We'll deal with the latter connection in Chapter 8, where we also cover specialized stereo components that integrate with iTunes.)

Computers have become far more audiocentric than they used to be, but manufacturers still take shortcuts with audio hardware to save space or lower cost. To make iTunes' audio quality shine, try routing its sound out of your computer through a cleaner channel. If this sounds too complicated, don't worry; there are a few options here, and one of them only requires $25, an open USB port, and opposable thumbs.

Get Cleaner Sound from Your Desktop and Laptop (via USB)

Thanks to the ubiquity of support for the USB audio spec in today's operating systems, you can slap a USB output on any computer to improve your sound quality without installing anything complicated. Another advantage is that you can swap these between computers at your convenience—wherever you need good sound.

TIP

When you switch to a better sound output, it'll make your sound better on speakers, home stereos, and headphones. Some options give you multiple outputs; with others, you'll still have to switch between your speakers and headphones the way you normally do.

CAUTION

If your desktop computer was designed for multimedia or gaming, it likely will not require a better sound output than the one that came with it. Spend your money on new speakers instead.

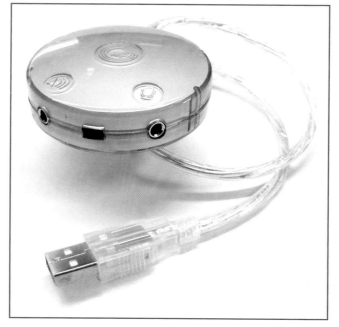

*Figure 5-11: **Dollar for dollar, you can't do much better sound-wise than Griffin Technology's iMic (average street price $35).***

The Griffin Technology iMic (Figure 5-11) is popular for a couple of reasons: it sounds great, and you can find it online from $25 to $40 or so. It has two jacks for inputting and outputting audio to your headphones, powered speakers, or stereo system. Budding home recording enthusiasts, archivists of records and cassettes, podcasters, and online radio DJs will enjoy the switch that lets you toggle between line- and mic-level input. Other than that, there are no controls; you probably won't even need to use the installer disc—that's how easy the iMic is to use with both kinds of USB (1.1 and 2). Another advantage is that it processes audio outside of your computer or laptop and so has to travel through less potentially interfering electrical fields.

To figure out if you need a new sound output, look for specs equal to or better than this: 90 dB S/N (decibel signal-to-noise ratio) and 0.05% THD (Total Harmonic Distortion). "Better," when it comes to sound cards and other audio outputs, means a higher S/N and a lower THD.

The iMic's 18-inch cord is too short to make it from the back of a desktop computer on the ground, so you might need to extend it with a USB hub. Luckily, the iMic works with every hub we've tested—even the one built into an old monitor stand. (A USB hub connects to one of your computer's USB ports and usually offers four or so ports where other devices, such as the iMic, can connect.)

There are several other external USB (and Firewire) audio interfaces to choose from; we're only mentioning the Griffin iMic here because it's so cheap and widely compatible. Poke around online for them by searching for *USB audio output*. Griffin also makes a product called PowerWave that might suit you better, since it can power speakers. Other manufacturers of USB audio devices suitable for use with iTunes include Turtle Beach, Creative, Harmon Kardon (their DAL-150 is discontinued but available), and Xitel.

Get Cleaner Sound from Your Desktop (via PCI Slot)

If you don't mind opening up your computer to install a card, consider upgrading your sound with a PCI sound card. It's not too hard, although it does involve grounding yourself against static, opening up your computer's case, and snapping a fragile circuit board into an empty PCI slot. See why we like the Griffin iMic so much?

Get Cleaner Sound from Your Laptop (via PCMCIA Slot)

If you travel a lot or want even better sound than the iMic out of your laptop (plus a dedicated volume dial), go with the ultracompact Echo Indigo

(Figure 5-12). We've never heard stronger or cleaner sound out of a laptop than while using one of these, and you'll barely know it's there due to the tiny size and cable-free design.

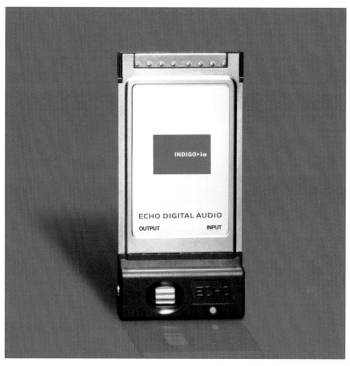

Figure 5-12: *The Echo Indigo gives you pristine stereo input and output.*

A six-foot cable for connecting to stereo or speakers comes as a standard accessory.

5

Chapter 6

Using the iPod for More Than Just Music

The iPod's main duty is providing a convenient way to listen to music, but you shouldn't forget that there's a computer and disc drive inside—after all, Apple developers never do. Just beneath the surface, within the menus of the iPod, are features for fun, as well as serious business. Applications that take advantage of the iPod's capabilities increase the benefits of carrying around the shiny little pod.

Could the iPod Replace Your PDA?

With so many different gadgets now competing for space in your bag (or if you're the type, on your belt), it's a relief that the iPod can take over the most compelling features of a Personal Digital Assistant (PDA) like the Palm or a Windows CE unit. Keeping contacts and calendar data close at hand while also providing some diversions in the form of games to play makes the iPod a funner and more reliable companion.

NOTE

Other than the QuickSteps sidebar on enabling the iPod to be accessed as an external drive, nothing in this chapter applies to the iPod Shuffle. It functions as advertised: as minimally as possible.

QUICKSTEPS

ENABLING ACCESS TO THE iPOD'S DISK

In order to take advantage of most of the iPod's extra features covered in the chapter, aside from the games, you'll need to expand the ability to write to the iPod's disk drive beyond the usual song transfer. This is easily accomplished.

1. Connect the iPod to your computer.

2. Select **Edit I Preferences** to open iPod preferences. Make sure the **iPod** tab in preferences is selected and the **Music** tab is selected under the iPod category.

3. Check the box next to **Enable Disk Use**.

If you've already chosen **Manually Manage Songs And Playlists** under the **Music** tab, **Enable Disk Use** will be selected automatically and will appear grayed out and unable to be changed.

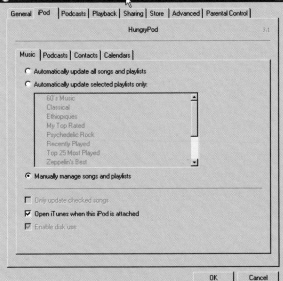

With games, alarms, notes, slideshows, and contacts, the iPod is also starting to converge with all the supercharged capabilities of top-of-the-line mobile phones. As we've seen with the new Motorola ROKR phone with iTunes capability, the convergence is here, and we won't be too suprised if one day soon we start hearing more about an actual iPod with phone capability.

But that's in the future. At the moment, you've got a handful of extra-musical features to master, so let's get started.

Use the iPod Calendar

The cool-looking calendar is a nice feature to have around to remind you of important events in your daily life. Don't get your hopes up too high though: it's not, sad to say, much of a PDA killer, and if you depend on an electronic calendar to keep track of your life, you'll probably still need your other gizmo to satisfy that demand.

The big shortcoming of the iPod Calendar (Figure 6-1), which is natural given the iPod's lack of a keyboard, is that you can't create or even edit data on the iPod itself. In other applications this lack is not so bad, but for someone with a lot of daily events and the

Figure 6-1: *The iPod Calendar looks good and is very handy, if rather feature-deprived.*

need to make changes on the fly, it's pretty crippling. On the other hand, if you usually just set appointments and stick with them, you can get by with what the iPod offers: about half the functionality of a PDA calendar.

At any rate it's free and easy enough to set up. Try playing with the Calendar and see if it suits your needs.

Once you've succeeded in loading your calendar, you'll want to display all the data that you've pulled in. One quite useful feature is the ability to keep multiple Calendar files and display them individually or all together (Figure 6-2).

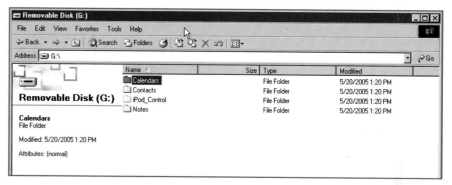

Figure 6-2: *The iPod Calendar is a convenient way to display your appointments. Just don't expect to edit them on the go from your iPod—for that you'll need to go back to your computer to move the files into their correct folder.*

Keep Contacts on the iPod

While it's usually a gateway to moments of sweet isolation, with your contacts on board, the iPod becomes a handy tool for staying in touch with others. Of course, you can't use it by itself for e-mail or phone calls, but if you want to have your contacts and addresses close at hand, the iPod is a handy solution. Because it connects with your computer it's easy to load up names, addresses, and other points of contact—often easier than the options available with your mobile phone.

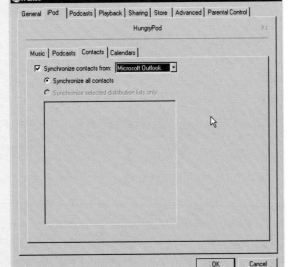

QUICKSTEPS

IMPORTING CONTACTS AND CALENDAR DATA FROM MICROSOFT OUTLOOK

With iTunes version 5.0 and later, importing contacts and calendar data from Microsoft Outlook is a snap. You can be grateful you didn't have to go through the old methods of hacking it, which were almost as bad as having to walk six miles in the snow to get to school.

1. Connect your iPod to your computer, and start iTunes.

2. Click the **iPod** tab and then the **Contacts** or **Calendars** tabs, depending on which one you want.

3. Click the checkbox next to **Synchronize Contacts From.**

4. Choose **Microsoft Outlook**, or **Outlook Express** from the dropdown menu.

5. Click **Synchronize All Contacts** (or **Selected Distribution Lists** if applicable).

6. Click the **Calendars** tab.

7. Click the checkbox next to **Synchronize Calendars From Microsoft Outlook.**

8. Click **OK.**

9. Your data will now be transferred to your iPod, and refreshed whenever you connect in the future.

Just as the iPod uses iCalendar and vCalendar formats to store event data, it uses the vCard format to store contacts. What that means for you is that this is the format in which you'll need to export your data. Also, as with the calendar programs, the multiplicity of various contacts programs is beyond this book's scope.

For Mac users, especially those using the built-in Apple contact and calendar programs, synchronizing is easy. For Windows users—particularly those who use Microsoft Outlook—what used to be a tricky process was cleaned up with iTunes version 5 and its greater support for importing data from Outlook. If you use other programs it might still be tricky, but if there's one thing to feel good about it's that for almost every program, as time goes on, so does proper integration of these standards.

LOAD CONTACTS IN WINDOWS

It's now very easy to get your contacts from Microsoft Outlook onto the iPod (see the Quicksteps sidebar).

CREATE A VCARD MANUALLY (WINDOWS)

If you want to create vCards to enter in your iPod's Contacts list on the Windows platform and you don't use Outlook, you're in for a bit of a hassle. One program we found that worked okay was the dubiously titled SuperCool PIM. You can run the program up to 30 times before you have to register for $30, and you can only enter 30 users. That's a lot of 30's, but it basically means you can use it to enter 30 names onto your iPod and then update that list up to 30 times for free if you play your vCards right.

1. Download SuperCool PIM from www.superbookmark.com (that's not a typo).

2. Select the directory where you wish to store your contacts database.

3. Log in as <u>Admin</u> and leave the password field blank.

4. Click the **New Contact** icon.

5. Explore the tabs; input information on the **General** tab and then—this part's important—choose to enter information in either the **Business** or **Home** tab. The iPod will only see **Name**, **Address**, **E-mail**, and **Phone**.

6. This is important: check the boxes for information you want to appear. Whether you choose the **Home** or **Business** tab, make sure the **Default** box in that tab is checked.

7. Enter all the information you want to about a person.

8. Click the **Save** and **Add** buttons when you're done entering the information for your first contact, and then continue entering contacts until you've entered 30 or run out of people you want to enter. Then, click **Save** and **Exit** to go back to the main screen.

9. To export the contacts as vCards, click the **All** button in the upper left of the main window in order to display all of your contacts. Select all of your contacts (click **All** in the left navigation bar, click the top name, hold the **Shift** key, and then click the bottom name).

10. Click the **Menu** button and choose **Export Records I To vCard File**.

11. In the next screen, in the **Range** field, click the **Export All The Records Displayed In Current Grid** button. In the box that pops up, navigate to your iPod's **Contacts** folder (**My Computer I Your iPod I Contacts**). This requires that your iPod be enabled for use as an external hard drive in **iPod Options**.

12. Click the **Export** button to send the contacts to your iPod.

It's Partially Fun and Games

If you're a games fanatic, you certainly shouldn't trade in your PSP or Gameboy for an iPod. Then again, if you're a music fanatic, you wouldn't trade your iPod for a slick games machine, either. And since you're carrying around your iPod, there's nothing wrong with playing a game of Brick or Solitaire to pass the time.

In fact, the recent addition of Music Quiz to the roster of iPod games is a pretty cool example of taking what the iPod does well and, well, making a game out of

TIP

If your contacts don't show up on your iPod after you import them, Apple recommends resetting your iPod (simultaneously hold down **Menu** and **Select**, the button in the middle of the scroll wheel).

QUICKSTEPS

PLAYING GAMES (GENERIC VERSION)

Since most of the games on the iPod are pretty self-explanatory, this is the quick version of getting your games up and running. If you need more detailed explanation of specific games, you'll find further information on them later in this chapter.

1. From the **iPod** menu, click **Extras I Games**.

2. This brings you to the **Games** menu. From here, choose the game you want.

3. Start playing.

4. To end the game, just click **Menu** on the scroll wheel, and you'll escape the game.

it! Playing random snippets of your own music collection, particularly if it's a large one, is a challenging variation on the old *Name That Tune* TV show.

Your selection of games depends on the iPod model you have, as well as the version of firmware installed. The games included in the current models are Solitaire, Brick, Parachute, and Music Quiz.

Bounce the Brick

Brick should be very familiar to anyone who grew up in America in the '70s and '80s because it's so similar to games like Breakout that were popular in video arcades and home machines. Even if you've never seen it, it's easy to pick up. Mastering it, however, can take a lifetime. Or not.

1. From the **iPod** menu click **Extras | Games | Brick**.
2. A screen appears with a few layers of blocks ("bricks") at the top and a longer, single block at the bottom (your paddle).
3. A small dot (the ball) is at the left side. Press the **center** button to begin, and the ball starts falling toward your paddle.
4. Move your paddle left or right using the **click wheel** and try to catch the ball, which will then bounce back to hit the bricks. Each time the ball hits a brick, it disappears. When you successfully wipe out one wall of bricks, another will pop up to take its place. If you miss hitting the ball, it falls away. You get three balls.

Shoot the Parachute

Parachute also takes its cue from old-time video games; in this case, the game is a lot like the old Missile Command genre: things fly overhead and your missile tower shoots them down before they can land.

1. From the **iPod** menu, click **Extras | Games | Parachute**.
2. Your missile tower is in the center bottom; take a few moments to practice your aim by using the scroll wheel.
3. Press the **center** button to begin.
4. Helicopters will begin to fly overhead, dropping parachutists down on you. Shoot all of them, especially the parachutists.

NOTE

Apple's general ban on third-party development for the iPod extends to the games arena, but that situation could change at some point in the future.

5. If a parachutist lands on your tower, it is destroyed and the game is over. Flying debris can also destroy your tower and end the game.

6. Points are added for every shot you make and deducted for anything missed.

Take the Music Quiz

Were you a fan of the TV show *Name That Tune*? If so, Music Quiz will be right up your alley. Even if you didn't like the TV show, you might like this, because the only music you'll hear is from your own collection (Figure 6-3).

1. Put your headphones on.

2. Click **Extras I Games I Music Quiz**.

3. A part of a song in your collection will begin playing at random as a list of songs from your collection appears on screen. The song playing is one of the titles.

4. Try to figure out which song is playing. Scroll up or down to choose which song you think is yours.

5. As you wait, some wrong choices are removed, one at a time, finally leaving you with the correct answer (and scoreless—points are based on how much time you take to answer correctly).

6. The game doesn't really end, it just goes on as you keep scoring. In addition to overall score, the game also keeps track of how many rounds you've played and how many you've won, so you can play again and work to improve your ratio.

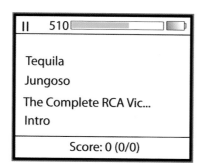

Figure 6-3: **Music Quiz plays a song from your collection at random and lets you pick out the title from a list of songs.**

Anything Else to Play?

The recent buzz is that Apple is looking to ramp up gameplay on the iPod soon. For the time being, for graphics-based games, you basically get what comes built-in.

There are now some third-party developers that are intent on making games for the iPod, but because of the tight grip Apple has on the iPod firmware, the games are best described as hacks. However, they're fun hacks: the offerings are mostly adventure-like games, based on text (sort of electronic versions of those "Choose Your Own Ending" books that used to be popular with early teens). Xoplay.com is the website of one such developer, offering a variety of fantasy games available for download.

SETTING THE ALARM

It's only fair to warn you, the alarm beep is not so loud. So if you're a heavy sleeper, we can't recommend relying on it for morning reveille. But for light sleepers or for other purposes it's quite functional.

1. From the **iPod** menu, click **Extras I Clock I Alarm Clock I Time**.

2. The **Alarm Time** menu will let you set the time you want your alarm to sound. Use the scroll wheel to adjust the time, and click the **center** button when it's correct.

3. You will be taken back to the **Alarm Clock** menu.

4. Turn the alarm on or off by clicking **Alarm**.

5. Set the sound you'd like the alarm to make, either a beep that sounds with no need for headphones, or one of your playlists that will start playing through the normal sound outlet, headphones, or your stereo if it's hooked up.

NOTE

Like many current features of the iPod, Notes wasn't always an option and seems to have been added partially because of the early hacks created by users who leveraged iPod contact files for other data. These users showed so much determination, it was proof of the need for a solution!

Set the Time

As many rap stars tell us, you're nothing if you don't know what time it is; iPods, friend, are here to help. First though, you have to set your time.

1. From the **iPod** menu, click **Extras I Clock I Date & Time I Set Time Zone**.

2. Scroll through the list of options for your particular region and click the **center** button to set your highlighted choice.

3. Click **Menu** on the scroll wheel once to go back, then scroll down and click **Set Date & Time**.

4. Use the scroll wheel to set the hour, then click the **center** button to set your choice. The next option will be selected automatically. Go through and set all options. When you've finished you'll be sent back to the **Date & Time** menu automatically.

5. From there, you can pick whether you want time displayed in 12-hour or 24-hour format. Just scroll down and click **Time** and change from 12 to 24 and vice versa.

6. If you want the time displayed more frequently, scroll down once more, choose **Time In Title**, and click it to turn it on. Activated, it will replace the title in most menus with the time, usually after a short delay during which the menu title is shown.

Maximize the Notes Feature

Deep within the hearts of technical nerds there is a special place for the plain text document. It's simple, and therein lies its power. From a note reminding you to bring home some olives, directions to the olive store, to the screenplay to the movie *Popeye*: you can store it all as a text note.

The Notes feature, which uses plain text, carries with it that same power and mystique. Enterprising pod users have hacked all sorts of things into the form of notes, even games. Still, basically, Notes is just a handy way of carrying around some text. It's up to you to make it powerful.

Load Notes onto Your iPod

One of the iPod's native abilities is to read text files, so putting a note onto it doesn't require any kind of conversion; you just save the text file into the **Notes** section of the iPod's hard drive.

1. Connect the iPod to your computer. (Make sure that disk use is enabled, as described earlier.)

2. Open **My Computer** and find the iPod listed as a drive.

3. Create a TXT file. In Windows, you can create it with Notepad, Wordpad, Microsoft Word, or any other text editing program that came with your computer—just remember to pick **File I Save As**.

4. Drag and drop any Notes files from your computer to the **Notes** folder.

Use iPod as Navigator

One of the most frequently used types of notes is traveling directions. Go to your favorite website for directions—mapquest.com, maps.google.com, maps.yahoo .com, or whatever—and when the directions surface, click the link for **Printable Version**. This will turn any graphics (such as Yahoo's icons for **R** and **L**) into plain text. Select the text, copy it into Notepad, edit it if necessary, and then save it to Notes on your iPod. Those directions take up negligible space on your iPod, so don't even bother erasing them, unless you have some other reason to.

Read Literature on Your iPod

For those of you who are interested in trying something literary—and testing your eyes to the limit—you can download works of classic literature in the plain text format (TXT) and save them onto the iPod using the Note creation technique. The iPod's screen is better suited to short notes, directions, addresses, and contacts, but it is possible to put longer text works on there as well.

iPOD3eBOOK

This is not easy, but if you follow the directions, it's relatively simple—even if you've never seen a DOS window before. iPod3eBook is a command-line program, meaning that the interface is as rudimentary as any you've ever seen and involves only a small range of text-based commands. If it doesn't work for you, you can use iPodSoft iStory Creator, covered next.

As with so many other features in this chapter, you'll need to have your iPod connected and enabled as an external drive for this to work.

1. Download the program after finding it (or try www.alphalink.com.au/~timmo) and unzip it to **My Computer | C Drive | iPod3ebook**.

2. Find the text file you wish to convert into iPod-readable chunks and put it into the **iPod3ebook** folder.

3. This is where it gets a little hairy. Go to the **Start** menu at the lower-left corner of Windows and click **Run**.

4. Type cmd in the window that pops up.

5. In the DOS window that pops up after that, type C:.

6. Type CD/ipod3ebook.

7. Type iPod3ebook NAME.txt (where NAME is the name of the file you want to slice up for iPod consumption).

8. In the **My Computer | C Drive | iPod3ebook** folder, you'll find a folder with the same file name as your TXT file. Copy the entire folder into your iPod's **Contacts** folder.

9. Unmount the iPod in the Windows taskbar by right-clicking it. Then disconnect the iPod from the cable.

10. Navigate to the folder on your iPod (**Main Menu | Extras | Notes**) and look for the folder you put there.

11. iPod3eBook automatically maxes each page out at 4K and adds links to next and previous pages at the top and bottom of each page when it displays on your iPod. Press the center **Select** button in the middle of the scroll wheel to jump forward and back between pages using the links.

iPODSOFT iSTORY CREATOR (MAC AND WINDOWS)

If you'd rather write your own story for perusal on your or other peoples' iPods, this program is the way to go. It's still in beta at this point, but it looks to be a reliable way to create "choose your own adventure"–style text games as well as other linked text documents that you can access via the iPod's Notes feature. Here's how.

1. Download the program from www.iPodsoft.com.

2. Unzip the installation files to a new folder on your **desktop**.

CAUTION

We wouldn't recommend trying to look up directions, quotations, or other notes on your iPod while driving. After you pull over to check, the iPod's backlight could come in handy.

TIP

One of the largest repositories for free works of literature in the public domain is Project Gutenberg (www.gutenberg.org).

CAUTION

We used a version of iPod3eBook that was a Windows compilation of the code by a third party. Search the Web for information on the program or others like it to find the latest version.

TIP

One of the advanced options in this program lets you name the title of the note so that it doesn't end up being called SOMETHING.txt on your iPod. To specify new names for the note, its folder, and its file name on your iPod, open the DOS window again and type ipod3ebook -t YOURTITLE -d YOURFOLDERNAME -f YOURFILENAME NAME.txt.

3. Double-click the application file called **iStoryInstall**.

4. Click **Next | Agree | Next | Next | Next | Close** to install the program.

5. The first time you use it, iStory Creator will ask you to enter your Name/Nickname and e-mail address (Figure 6-4). iPodSoft says it only uses this information for when you submit an iStory to their central area, for administrative purposes.

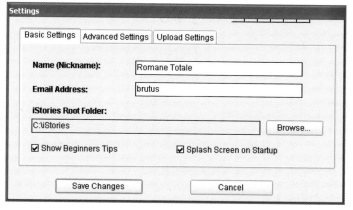

*Figure 6-4: **Enter your basic information here so that iPodSoft can e-mail you should you upload your piece, and so that you'll get credit for the story/text game.***

6. Click the **Browse** button next to the **iStories Root Folder** text field. On the next screen, click your **C drive** and then the **New Folder** button; call the new folder iStories, select it, and click **OK**.

7. Click **Save Changes** to exit the **Settings** menu (you can return at any time by clicking **Tools | General Options**).

8. Click the **New Story** button (Figure 6-5) and then fill out the **Story Title** in the window that pops up.

9. Add a **Page Title** to your first page—something descriptive. As for the **Page Comments** field, the reader won't see that; it's for you to keep your pages organized using the left pane (the Comments text shows up there).

10. Start writing your story in the top field, underneath the title (Figure 6-6). If you have the story/game written somewhere else, you can paste it in.

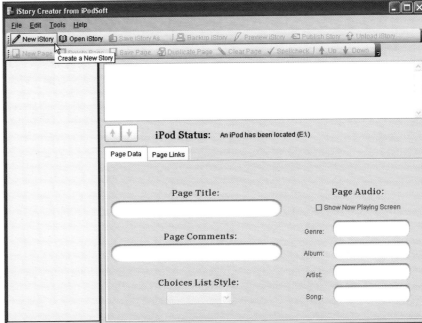

Figure 6-5: *Every good story starts with a click of the mouse.*

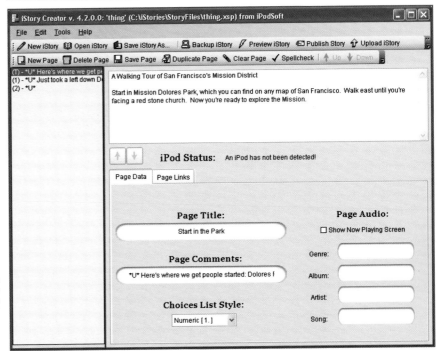

Figure 6-6: *Now we're cooking; I have the first page of my adventure just about filled out.*

11. Unbelievably, you can even pick a Genre, Album, Artist, or Song to play as the user reads this page. We recommend filling out only one of these fields, preferably Song (and get the spelling right).

12. Click over to the **Page Links** tab. Double-click the prefilled **Choice** text, and type in your own (Figure 6-7).

13. Figure out which page you want that particular **Choice** on page 1 to link to (Figure 6-7). It can be helpful to chart the flow of your adventure/story on a physical piece of paper, just to keep things straight. However, you won't enter the linking information now, since the other pages don't exist yet; you choose from a drop-down menu of existing pages.

14. You've got the idea now; keep creating your story. When it's done, click the **Publish Story** button to create a Zip file of your story that can be uploaded or downloaded to or from the Web, e-mailed around, traded on file sharing networks, etc.

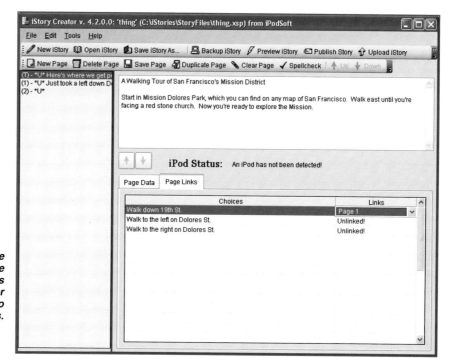

*Figure 6-7: **Once I create the other pages, I'll be able to choose them in this drop-down menu in order to assign the Choices to specific pages.***

15. To share your story with others on the Story message boards, click the **Upload iStory** button. Both the **Publish Story** and **Upload iStory** buttons can be seen in the preceding figures.

Clearly, this format's a little constricting, but you might find that it provides enough structure for some pretty far-out ideas. Maybe you'll make millions creating audio-visual tours of the island of Maui using only iStory Creator, your own custom music, and the fact that so many people travel with iPods.

For Color-Screen iPod Owners Only

When iPod Photo was first released, it struck many observers as overkill. The need for a pocket-sized photo viewer just didn't justify spending the extra bucks. Time, however, is looking more kindly on Apple's decision, as a convergence of factors makes photos on the iPod more useful and appealing.

Import and Display Photos

The growing popularity of digital photography, combined with the growth of ever-greater megapixel cameras, means that a convenient, portable storage unit for pictures is becoming a must-have. Fortunately for Apple (and for iPod owners) the ability to use the iPod as a photo vault, accomplished with the Camera Connector, is a big boost for usefulness. On a vacation, nothing beats the ability to snap as many photos as you want without worrying about running out of flash memory.

Once the photos are loaded, displaying them is so easy we don't even need to take you through the steps. From the **iPod** menu just click **Photos** and you'll see a list of your picture folders (Figure 6-8). Choose one and soon you'll see thumbnails (they're actually smaller—pinkynails?) of everything in the folder. Use the scroll wheel to click the photo you wish to display, or click **Play** to see them all as a slideshow.

TIP

If you want to display your pictures on a television screen, you'll want them looking sharp, so make sure to import them at **Full Resolution**.

QUICKSTEPS

IMPORTING PHOTOS FROM YOUR COMPUTER

You can set your iPod to sync with iTunes for pictures as well as music. It's just as easy.

1. Connect iPod to your computer.

2. Click **Edit I Preferences** and make sure the **iPod** tab is selected in the **Preferences** dialog box.

3. Choose the **Photos** tab.

4. Check **Synchronize My Photos From** and choose the folder. (**My Pictures** is the default.)

5. Decide if you'd like all photos copied or just particular folders, then click the appropriate choice.

6. If you decide to import only from selected folders, you must check those you wish to import from. A full listing of the folders in the top chosen directory (for instance, **My Pictures**) is displayed, along with the number of pictures contained within each folder.

7. Decide if you want to select the **Include Full-Resolution Photos** option. This is important if you plan to display the photos on a TV or other large-size screen where you'll need high resolution. If you don't plan on doing this, carrying around high resolution images is just a waste of disc space; without this option checked, iTunes will resize the photos it copies to the iPod at a resolution appropriate for its 220 x 176–pixel resolution screen.

CAUTION

Be sure to have a good charge on your battery when you import photos. Sometimes, especially with large-resolution cameras, it can be a big drain.

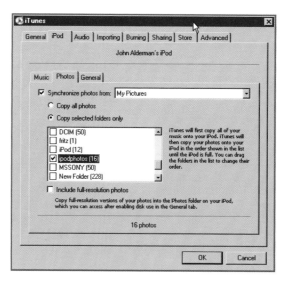

Figure 6-8: **The subdirectories of your photo folder are displayed, so you can choose which ones you want synched with the iPod.**

Get the Camera Connector

The Apple Camera Connector is a handy new accessory for the iPod that retails for around $30. While it supports a wide range of cameras that have USB connections, there is a limited number that Apple officially supports, so check before buying. If your camera isn't on the list, you might want to buy it anyway, but be sure to keep your receipt and that your store takes returns.

Using the Connector is very easy: you just attach it to your iPod and plug in your camera with its USB cable. Your iPod then copies all of the photos in your camera, as well as movies (though it can't display these). Finally, you are given the option of erasing your camera's storage.

We think the Connector is another example of Apple creating a simple, useful product. And in this case, Apple's version is less than half the price of competitors.

QUICKSTEPS

IMPORTING PHOTOS USING THE iPOD CAMERA CONNECTOR

Apple includes software for dealing with the Apple iPod Camera Connector in the software for iPod itself.

1. Snap the connector into your iPod dock.

2. Connect your camera to the Camera Connector using the standard USB-to-USB mini cable your camera came with. (If you don't have one, pick one up from any computer supply store.)

3. That's it! The photos will start uploading from your camera to your iPod, where they'll form a new photo album.

Present Slideshows to Go

So you've got a pocket full of pictures. Now, what can you do with them? You put on a show! The iPod lets you display your photos in a series, with professional-style transitions. Perhaps best of all, you can designate a playlist as the soundtrack, so that if your audience gets bored by your trip to Miami, at least they'll be able to groove along with your choice of tunes.

1. From the **iPod** menu, click **Photos | Slideshow Settings**. This will bring up a large menu of variables for you to pick from.

2. Click **Time Per Slide** and choose how long you'd like each image displayed before moving on to the next.

3. Click **Music** and choose whether you want music or not; if you do, choose which of your playlists should be the source.

4. Choose **Repeat** if you'd like to keep the slideshow going continuously.

5. Turn on **Shuffle Photos** if you want a random sequence. (Together with the last option, you can set up an interesting party atmosphere.)

6. Click **Transitions** to choose which type of transition to use to slide from one picture to the next, or turn it off if you want straight slideshow style.

7. Turn on **TV Out** if your slideshow will be displayed on your TV (more on that later).

8. Set **TV Signal** for the type of TV you'll be using. (NTSC is the American standard, PAL the European.)

9. Finally, from the **Photo** menu, choose the folder you want to use for the slideshow, or choose **Photo Library** if you want everything you've got, and click **Play**. The slideshow will begin, set to the music of your choice.

Chapter 7
Supercharging Your iPod

The iPod on its own, fresh from the box, is a great self-contained system. Its advantages are many, and we don't need to go over them again here. One point worth noting is this: because the iPod is a very sophisticated piece of design, it has a lot of latent potential. The interface is simple and compelling enough that a clever addition can boost power in any number of ways—some quite ingenious. When you bought it you might have thought you were just getting a handy walkabout to play music for yourself, but with a few add-ons you could end up with a block-rocking mega-system, with your trusty little iPod at the heart of it, supplying the tunes.

This chapter is all about those things that you can add to expand the range of your iPod just a little beyond itself, and while we're at it we'll also briefly cover accessories such as cases and carrying bags.

Speaker Setups

Your iPod comes with headphones, and we covered several other headphone options in Chapter 5. At the other extreme, you can use the iPod to power your home entertainment system's audio, which we'll cover in the next chapter. This section, however, deals with those situations that fall smack dab in the middle of headphones and big home setups. Whether portable or for the home, small or not so small, these speaker setups have built-in amplifiers, so all they require is an iPod and some power, either from batteries or a wall outlet.

Rugged Portable Speakers

Here, we could have included a bunch of those little speaker systems that lack amplification, and so don't require batteries. You can find those in a wide variety of stores, and their chief advantage is that you're not going to get too upset about destroying $15 speakers. None of them sound good enough to warrant inclusion in this book—we're trying to show you how to get good results from your iPod. That's why we recommend only using speakers that require additional voltage from a wall power outlet or batteries; otherwise your sound will be tinny and weak.

You can use some of the indoor portable speakers we suggest in the next section in the outdoors, but if you're going to be doing a lot of camping or picnicking or go on other outdoor audio adventures, you want something tough enough to stand up to the task. A good option is the Digital Lifestyle Outfitters iBoom (www.dlodirect.com).

Slide your iPod into the center slot, and it becomes the nervous system of the iBoom (Figure 7-1). While docked in the iBoom, the iPod's controls are nicely exposed on the front; you can use them as you normally would to navigate and control menus. The iBoom's own controls handle volume and add FM radio controls (two presets and a digital tuner with a little LCD). It handles all dockable iPods and iPod Minis and runs on AC power or six D batteries.

CAUTION

Although the iBoom is designed to be rugged and add some shock resistance to the iPod it's carrying, it's not very water resistant and you still don't want to bang it around too much. Digital Lifestyle Outfitters also offers a bag that adds another layer of protection.

TIP

You can use the DLO iBoom to charge your iPod or iPod Mini. Just attach the iPod as usual and it will draw power from the iBoom's supply, whether that's batteries or alternating current from the wall.

TIP

If you want to plug an iPod Nano into a speaker system designed for the iPod in general (as opposed to specifically for the Nano), you'll need to use the dock adapter that came with your Nano. If you lost it, you can order another from Apple.com.

Figure 7-1: **The iPod fits easily into the center slot of the iBoom, where it becomes the brain of the unit.**

Ultra-Portable Speakers

The iBoom's on the large side, as are many of the speakers in the next section. If you're looking for a way to deploy decent-sounding iPod speakers from as small a bag as possible, we recommend the Creative TravelSound i300 (Figure 7-2). Running 35 hours on four AAA batteries, this tiny two-speaker system folds up and fits into a black Velcro bag. Plus, it brings cleaner highs and punchier lows than the competition.

Portable Home Speakers

If you're looking for something a little more stylish for use in the home with a larger size and docking station for your iPod but don't want to commit yourself

Figure 7-2: *The Creative TravelSound i300 sounds better than its small size would have you believe.*

to setting up a fully wired (or wireless) system, consider the Altec Lansing inMotion or the Bose SoundDock. Both of these offer good looks and iPod-specific compatibility.

There's a big price jump between the inMotion and the SoundDock, as well as a jump in sound quality. The SoundDock is about twice the price, so your budget may have final say. The nice thing is that it's easy to upgrade later; the same iPod can rest comfortably at the heart of any future system.

Semiportable Speakers

The best-sounding dedicated iPod speaker system we've heard so far is the Altec Lansing inMotion iM7. Its large tubular design affords excellent sound

Figure 7-3: **The Altec Lansing inMotion iM7 is worth the $250 asking price if you're looking for a fair compromise between sound and portability.**

with that extra thump only a subwoofer can provide (it's on one end). Any dockable iPod docks into the smooth, spring-loaded built-in iPod cradle with a satisfying snap, and you get an IR remote control for basic playback functions. An AC adapter makes it a great home stereo, or you can lug it to the beach thanks to the hidden battery compartment that houses a full battery of D-cell batteries.

That excellent sound will cost you in the areas of portability and price, however; the inMotion iM7 weighs 12 pounds and costs $250 (Figure 7-3). But considering that it can be used as an analog stereo input for your computer, TV, VCR, DVD player, radio, or non-iPod MP3 player and also considering this unit's stellar sound, that price could well be worth it. It even hosts an S-video output for running slideshows from your iPod.

iPod Speaker Setups for the Home

If you already have a stereo system or home entertainment system, you can hook your iPod up to it quite easily (see Chapter 8). The self-contained, amplified speaker systems we're covering here, on the other hand, can be used in conjunction with an iPod in place of a full-fledged sound system. Put one of these in a room that lacks a system, and it'll lack no longer. There are two main types: the larger, full-sounding variety that are designed to be left in one place, and the modular, portable systems designed for one room.

2.1-STEREO SYSTEMS

While it's nice to enjoy the personal pleasures and increased sense of musical immediacy that headphone listening allows, the room-filling warmth and excitement that a good set of stereo speakers brings is about as pleasing a way to relax (or rock out) as there is. Setting up a decent pair of speakers to your iPod is a great way to get a more physical sense of music.

There are quite a few speaker sets that work well with the iPod both for sound and visual appeal. Creative's I-Trigue Line, JBL CreatureSpeakers, and Harmon Kardon's Sound Sticks, or the Klipsch iFi iPod 2.1 (Figure 7-4) are all good candidates. Hooking them up is very easy, as is moving them around.

5.1- OR 7.1-CHANNEL SURROUND SOUND SYSTEMS

Surround sound systems are mostly associated with DVD players and high-end gaming computers, but hooked up to the iPod they can give your music that same mind-bending sense of your world coming alive from every direction. Plop your iPod down into a dock on top of your surround sound system that's hooked up to a spare analog input with a Y cable, and your surround sound system will be able to play it over all of the speakers. Experiment with Stadium, Hall, Simulated Surround, and other presets to find one that sounds good to you.

> **TIP**
>
> If some of the following speaker systems look familiar, that could be because these are the same speakers many people use with their computers. If you have any old computer parts lying around, you might consider harvesting powered speakers and trying them out with your iPod. That way, you can have amplified iPod music in lots of different locations.

> **NOTE**
>
> The ".1" in 2.1-, 5.1-, and 7.1-channel speaker systems stands for the subwoofer. So a 2.1-channel setup has three speakers: two stereo satellite speakers and one subwoofer.

Figure 7-4: **The Klipsch iFi iPod 2.1 Speaker System does the competition one better by offering a slick docking station for any dockable iPod and a wireless remote.**

Put Your iPod in Your Car

Using your iPod in your car is pretty amazing—it's like discovering the joys of an iPod all over again. Suddenly you have your entire music collection at your disposal while you're on the move.

We give the car installation a special treatment, so turn to the Appendix for our tips for hotwiring your car (not literally).

Portable Amplifiers: For the Audiophile Only

High-impedance headphones (high-performance, big over-the-ear headphones, that is) need juice. The iPod has lots of it but if you're going to use some big daddy phones, you're going to need even more juice, to improve sound and battery life.

A good source for all of your headphone amp needs (and you didn't know you had those, did you?) is Headphone.com. From $150 to over $5000, this is a great way to accentuate the distance between you and the audio riffraff—or just get some good sound from those mighty phones you've been carrying with a portable headphone amplifier.

iPod-Integrated Clothes

Of course, the most obvious place for your iPod is your pocket, purse, backpack, or shoulder bag. Pockets are built-in, require no extra money, and are not likely to be left behind somewhere (Figure 7-5). Purses and the others are a little roomier and comfortable, but do require some fumbling to find you your Pod in a pinch.

For true convenience, as well as sartorial splendor, you might want to check out some clothing designed with iPod use in mind. When one of the authors was a suit-wearing salary man in Tokyo (really), he always carried the iPod in his suit inner pocket, and it seemed like the perfect place for it. While so far no forward-looking suit designers have made custom iPod designs, there are some clothing makers that have music on their minds. The result: a bevy of action-oriented gear that's friendly to your unit (Figure 7-6 and Figure 7-7).

Figure 7-5: **The Burton Shield iPod Jacket (www.burton .com) has Playback and Volume controls on its sleeve. We're trying really hard to resist adding some sort of pun about having tricks up one's . . . oh, never mind.**

Figure 7-6: *Scott eVest (www.scottevest.com) has a number of jackets and bags that hide cables, and in some cases even recharge your iPod with a solar panel on your back.*

Figure 7-7: **The Burton Amp Pack is part of the company's 2005 urban bag line and has the same controls found on the jacket. It's far less expensive and can be used with any other jackets you might have.**

Carrying Cases

Apple sells cases for every iPod on its website, including an official sock for keeping your player scratch-free. But to individualize your look, there's a healthy market of iPod case designers ranging from goofballs selling harebrained contraptions on the Web to high-end fashion designers hawking iPod cases that cost hundreds of dollars.

Apple's Case

This Spartan affair (Figure 7-8) obscures everything except the Hold switch on most iPods, but it includes a clip for belts or bag straps. Apple's case goes well with an inline (wired) remote control.

Apple's Armband

Apple smartly doesn't recommend that people jog every day with a heavy 60GB iPod Photo. That's why it only sells armbands for the iPod Mini and iPod Shuffle lines. If you want to get technical about it, the Shuffle's the safest way to go, since it has no moving parts. But Apple has stated that if you use the armband with the Mini, your body provides a certain degree of shock absorption (it's definitely better than using the included belt clip).

The armbands for Mini and Shuffle cost $29 each. You can also find armbands for these players sold by the third-party case manufacturers mentioned elsewhere in this section.

Figure 7-8: *Apple includes this durable, utilitarian case with some models and not others; if you don't have one, it will cost you $29.*

Custom Setups for Best of Class

When you want to build up your iPod for a particular activity, accessories can be tailored to fit your goals. This is one of the most powerful things about the iPod: its flexibility and knack for fitting in under very different situations.

This section is kind of a departure from the rest of the book. We're sticking with the style of the book, but these are more like suggestions of ways to customize and accessorize the iPod you own to be a unique tool that's suited for various activities.

Are You Experimental Jet Set?

Hopping from the cafes of Venice to the towers of Shanghai? It sounds glamorous, but the seasoned traveler knows that even the best itinerary has its

QUICKSTEPS

BUILDING A WORLD TRAVELER iPOD

If you have a trimode cell phone for answering calls the moment you set foot in Milan, you'll appreciate this setup. As one of the authors' grandfather once said, "Never be separated from your equipment"; when you're talking about the following selection of gear, it's good advice to keep in mind.

- Get the Apple World Traveler Adapter Kit. With this, the electrical outlets of most countries of the world are open to you, or rather your iPod. (You'll want to confirm before you start your globe-trotting, however, that the country you're going to is actually covered—while most are, you don't want any bad surprises.)

- Add a pair of noise-canceling or inner ear headphones. A set of noise-canceling headphones offers a peaceful audio sanctuary that can make all the difference between arriving in relaxed calm or frazzled irritation. Inner ear phones also keep a lot of the noise out and are all-around great. Your call.

- Download some essential foreign language lessons from Audible.com and polish up on whichever foreign tongue you'll be using in your destination. Nothing says uncouth tourist more than not even being able to thank your hosts in their own language. With the ability to take those language lessons with you, you have no excuse not to learn.

- With all the bumpy riding you'll want a rugged case. It's your choice if you want to pick one for style, but for rugged durability the Casemandu (http://www.casemandu.com/) is hard to beat. The manufacturer calls it "waterproof, dust proof, and shock proof," and it does seem very sturdy, if a tad bulky.

dull moments, when the kids on the flight are whining and the second-rate movie annoys more than entertains. Slipping into a relaxing world where you control the sounds (as detailed here in the QuickSteps sidebar) can be a lifesaver.

Get Physical

As we mentioned previously, due to the difference in what it uses to store music, the best iPod for physical activity is definitely the Shuffle. Our advice to those who like to sweat while they rock is to get a Shuffle and accessorize it with a strap like the SportWrap from XtremeMac (www.xtrememac.com) and then hit the gym (or the slopes, or whatever).

But say you just bought a standard or a Photo iPod, and you still want to work out. Well you're in luck, because there are some accessories that can help you. Read on, my friend.

BUILD AN EXERCISE FREAK iPOD

If you've ever tried to get or stay in shape, you know that nothing keeps you going like a pounding beat. In fact, we've heard that a certain fitness trainer in Los Angeles plans on marketing an MP3 player that keeps time with her kickboxing routine. That's still a bit far-fetched; for now, you'll have to settle for creating your own customized high-energy playlists for the gym, road, or dojo. Here's how to outfit your iPod (particularly the Mini, Nano, and Shuffle) for the occasion.

1. Buy an armband or carrying case that suits your individual taste. If you're going to be using your iPod Shuffle at the gym a lot, a necklace-style lanyard approach could work well, but for activities that entail more bouncing, an armband or carrying case with a belt clip works better. You might check these locations for more information on exercise-ready iPod cases:

   - www.speckproducts.com
   - www.iskin.com
   - www.apple.com (of course)
   - Any electronics store that sells the iPod

2. There are several podcasts now available aimed at the fitness market: try http://strengthradio.com/ or http://www.marinaspodcast.com/. Neither are free, but they might be interesting. (We cover the downloading of podcasts in Chapter 9.)

3. Make sure you have the right headphones. In general, you want lightweight headphones with a relatively short cord. Some people prefer earbud-style headphones that clip around the ear or behind the ear, while others like a medium-sized open-backed over-the-head headphone that allows them to hear traffic. Headphones, perhaps more than any other piece of technology, are largely a matter of personal taste, so while sound quality, a lightweight design, and out-of-the-way cables are all things to look for, your own comfort should be the main factor in your decision.

4. If possible, choose headphones that have replaceable earbuds or headphone covers.

iPods for Sound Snobs

While there are still some curmudgeons who bemoan the passing of the LP and analog stereo, for us the many advantages and conveniences of digital music—especially its ability to spread decent sound quality at a low price—earn it high marks in our book. For every high-end hi-fi snob in the good old days, there were a lot more terrible-sounding budget stereos, and those are pretty much a thing of the past. However, for those who want to bring back some of that snobbishness and become delicate-eared dilettantes, we offer the advice in "Building an iPod for Audiophile Bliss" for putting together a iPod system that will sound really good.

A Standby for Shutterbugs

One of the great things about having a machine with a lot of latent potential is that it can be developed in surprising directions. Who'd have thought that the iPod would turn out to be the unexpected companion to a growing legion of digital photographers? It may not yet be perfect—a professional will probably want a dedicated digital photo vault—but it's a solid step in that direction. And if you've already got the camera and the iPod, connecting the dots between them can sweeten the whole arrangement.

TURN YOUR iPOD INTO A PHOTOGRAPHER'S ASSISTANT

The iPod Photo was designed with photography in mind, so it doesn't take much to turn it into an excellent companion for just about any digital camera with a USB connection (there's a full compatibility chart on Apple.com).

1. Start with an iPod and a digital camera with a USB connection.

2. Buy the Apple iPod Camera Connector, which will let you upload your photos from your camera to the iPod, thus turning it into a digital photo vault. (Test the connector before you leave, because many cameras are not officially supported but work fine; testing will avoid any surprises.)

3. If you'll be taking the iPod along on possibly rough-and-tumble location shoots, you'll want to invest in a sturdy case.

4. If you like to give slideshows of your photos, you might want to invest in the naviPro eX remote control unit. This latest version of a dependable unit offers the ability to control slideshows as well as songs.

5. To keep up on the latest photo techniques, you can download the podcasts from www.tipsfromthetopfloor.com, which offer "tips & tricks for the digital photographer."

6. Since you want to look like a real photographer, you might want to get a field vest and stuff it full of your camera gear and your iPod. Vests from Domke are reputable and contain a whopping 18 pockets; the jackets (with zip-off arms) have 16.

Underwater iPod Listening

Before you dismiss this option out of hand for its seeming absurdity, trust us when we say that it is possible to put your iPod into a waterproof case, secure it to your person, swim to depths of up to 10 feet, and return to the edge of a pool without damage to iPod or limb. To avoid wardrobe malfunctions, you might spring for the optional swim belt accessory, which is also less likely to result in a missing iPod.

Underwater headphones get a bit tricky—sometime a manufacturer will sell waterproof cases but no headphones to go with them. Aside from the intuitive fact that normal headphones don't do well underwater, there are also water's different aural properties to contend with. That's why we went with the H2O

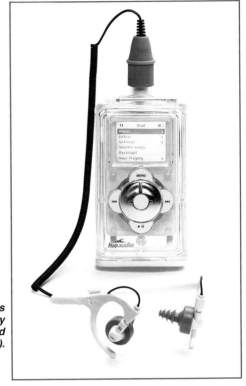

CAUTION

The iPod won't float when it's in the H2O Audio case, so keep track of it when you're swimming or engaging in other water sports. Also, use common sense when you wear these; you don't want to miss a cruise ship's foghorn while you're paddling along in an ocean kayak rocking to the oldies.

Figure 7-9: **H2O Audio SV offers waterproof cases for every generation of iPod (1G–4G, Photo, and Mini).**

Audio SV (Figure 7-9). It comes with waterproof headphones (actually, they're closer to head-mounted speakers) with a special jack that screws onto the case to form a seal.

Be an iPod DJ

There's no doubt that the glamour of being a DJ has soared to rarefied heights over the last decade. With all the music in your iPod burning a hole in your pocket, it's natural that you'd want to get in on the action and entertain your friends and fellow music heads with your great selection. Lucky for you, a little sweat and a few tools can help you do just that, and you can join like-minded Pod jockeys around the globe in getting parties moving and booties shaking.

QUICKSTEPS

LIVING THE LIFE AQUATIC WITH YOUR iPOD

There are a few ways to waterproof the iPod, but due to the elegant way in which H20 deals with the underwater headphone situation, we went with the H20 Audio SV Series for the iPod. It also lets you control your iPod underwater—even the scroll wheel.

1. Find the right case for your iPod on www.h2oaudio .com. Currently, supported models are the SV iMini (for the iPod Mini), SV iP3G (for the 3G iPod), and SV iP4G (for the 4G iPod); other models might be supported at a later date.

2. After charging your iPod, follow the instructions to secure the iPod in the case. You might as well try it out in a sink or bathtub before hitting the beach or pool to make sure you've got everything set up properly. Again, when you're submerging your iPod in water, it's no time to skip over the included instructions.

3. Consider the swim belt accessory if you're planning on doing serious snorkeling, or if you're worried about losing your iPod underwater.

4. One side benefit: your iPod is now waterproof for wet days on the downhill slopes or cross country ski trails this winter.

You've been reading along and eyeing the gear mentioned, but if you're like us, you kind of dread having to sink even more money into your hobby. We divided this bunch into two categories—amateur and semipro—so you won't get overwhelmed if you just want to test the waters.

BE AN AMATEUR iPOD DJ

This method works great if you want to have a preloaded DJ mix on your iPod, replete with crossfades from one song to another and other fancy moves you can add in. Your DJ mix will play all the way through if left unattended, which is the desired effect in most cases.

1. Get an audio editing program, and learn to use it. Audacity (http://audacity .sourceforge.net/) is a free open-source audio editing program that delivers surprisingly good quality. Though this is a powerful tool, learning to use it is not so hard (there are more tutorials on the website).

2. Open your songs for the night in your editing tool and patch them together into one big file, using crossfading, delay, repetition, and whatever other effects you want to throw in there. Mixing in movie quotes works well too, although it's illegal to download those from fan sites without permission of the copyright owner.

3. Once all the tracks are lined up end to end, mix the file down and put it on your iPod. Now when you play this file from your iPod over your own stereo or at the club, bar, pool room, campfire, or wherever, you'll have a solid evening of pumping entertainment.

4. Build up your library of dance tunes with tracks from DJ-oriented sites and labels (such as www.city16.com, www.FadeRecords.com, www.RatRecords.info) that offer digital downloads.

5. The iTunes Music Store is another good source for theme playlists you can purchase, but those cannot be edited into your mix in Audacity; you'd have to play them back-to-back, sans crossfading instead.

If you want something more hands-on, something that approaches the live shuffling of discs and the ability to choose tracks that move with the crowd's energy, you're going to need two iPods to allow you to seamlessly fade and keep the choices dynamic.

BE A SEMIPRO iPOD DJ

1. Buy a couple iPods so that you can seamlessly fade from one song to another. (Be sure you have duplicates of your songs on each one—or at least know which is which).

2. Get a mixing board. Nothing fancy here, just one of the kind record DJs have (and if you're always DJ-ing venues, chances are they'll have an in-house mixer)—something that will let you mix your iPods. The Tascam XS3 2-Channel Scratch DJ Mixer seems to be a good low-cost choice. For more frills, add real-time hardware effects with a Chaos Pad (touchpad) or D-Beam (sort of like a theremin).

3. If you're going to talk (like an old-school emcee) get a microphone. Most mixers have a mic input.

4. Practice at home with this setup until you get good at it. You still can't do tricks like scratching, but if someone makes an off-the-wall request you're a lot more likely to have it with you.

5. Read "Be an Amateur iPod DJ" for good sources of DJ-friendly tunes.

Be Organic

The iPod's a high-tech device, but that doesn't mean that you can't be environmentally sensitive with your choice of accessories, does it? We thought we'd finish off with an environmentally responsible iPod setup.

BUILD AN ORGANIC iPOD OUTFIT

1. Get an all-wood case from www.peterkinne.com/.

2. Pick up a portable solar battery charger for your iPod. It's environmentally sound and has a stylish triptych folding. (Find it at www.solio.com.)

3. Load up your iPod with the amazing field recordings of Bernie Krause. Soon you'll be grooving to the hypernatural sounds of the desert, forest, and ocean. At home on the planet.

NOTE

If you take any old iPod to the Apple store, they'll give you 10 percent off your next iPod and you can rest easy knowing that the chemicals in the iPod's battery and chips aren't leaching into the water supply.

How To...

Chapter 8
Playing Music at Home

People without iPods can get iTunes for free, but that doesn't mean it's not the best iPod accessory you already have. As you know by now, it's great for music playback at the computer, but with the right gear—all of it fairly inexpensive—you can turn iTunes into the brains behind a multiroom audio system that pipes tunes to your existing stereo equipment. If you're looking to add music to a kitchen, bedroom, or anywhere else in your living space, iTunes' ability to pipe digital music to inexpensive powered speakers can put audio in any room.

We covered sound cards and USB audio outputs back in Chapter 5, and you've been listening to iTunes over your computer speakers and headphones for a while now. Let's take a look at the best ways to play your iTunes and iPod music in one or more rooms of your house using stereo equipment, cables, and/or a wireless network.

Simple iTunes-to-Stereo Connection

If you live in a small space and have only one computer that's relatively close to your stereo system, this is the only section of this chapter you need. Here's how to use your computer as just another audio component, like a CD player on steroids.

Computer-to-Stereo Analog Connection

Connecting your desktop or laptop to a nearby stereo is easy, as long as the two are no more than about six feet apart.

1. Locate your computer's sound output. On desktops, this is often at the back (Figure 8-1); laptops usually have them on one of the sides (Figure 8-2). It's the same port you plug your headphones or computer speakers into.

Figure 8-2: **You've most likely already found the sound output on your laptop, but just in case you haven't, it's here.**

TIP

If your computer and stereo are really far apart but you don't want to get into any of the networking equipment discussed later in this chapter, Xitel's shielded High Definition RCA Extension Cable (www.xitel.com, $20) can add 30 feet to your Y-cable. Xitel says you can string them up to 90 feet from computer to stereo, but at that distance we recommend the AirPort Express (more on that later).

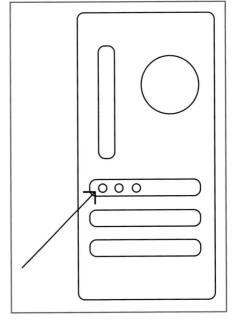

Figure 8-1: **The sound outputs on the back of a typical desktop computer**

TIP

Buy cable fasteners from just about any electronics store to route cable along the bottoms of walls and the backs of bookshelves. This minimizes the appearance of wires. Running them under rugs is another handy trick.

NOTE

If you have vinyl records, mix tapes, or radio shows you've been dying to hear in iTunes and on your iPod, the necessary connection is very similar to the simple computer-to-stereo connection just described.

QUICKSTEPS

SWITCHING BETWEEN SOUND OUTPUTS (WINDOWS)

If you have multiple sound outputs—for example, a sound card connected to your computer speakers and your USB audio output connected to your stereo—you'll often find yourself having to switch between the two. Here's how, in Windows (we'll get to the Mac steps soon).

1. Double-click the **speaker** icon in the system tray.

2. In the **Options** menu, choose **Properties**.

3. Select the device you want to use for playback from the **Mixer Device** drop-down menu at the top of the **Properties** window.

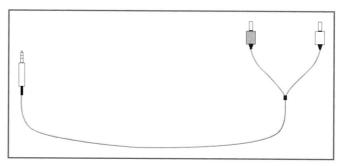

Figure 8-3: **The Y-cable is the most useful of all the cables. It bridges the gap between computers/iPods and stereo equipment.**

2. Insert the 1/8th-inch stereo plug on one end of the Y-cable (Figure 8-3) into your computer's output, whether it's a built-in sound output or an external USB one.

3. Connect the red and white plugs at the other end of the Y-cable to the corresponding red and white **Aux In** jacks on the back of your stereo system. You can use any open input except the one for **Phono**.

4. Select **Aux In** on your stereo (unless you plugged the Y-cable into one of the other jacks).

5. Click the **Play** button in iTunes.

6. How does it sound? If the sound is muddy or the volume's way off, set iTunes and your System Tray volume to about 75 percent, and then raise the volume knob on your stereo up from zero. If you don't find a setting that produces sound that's about as good as your CD player's, the problem could be your sound card. See Chapter 5 for replacement sound cards and USB audio sound card alternatives.

7. If you hear a hum along with your music, that means you've completed a connection from your computer to your stereo between two power outlets that have an electrical differential. The Ground Loop Isolator from Xitel (Figure 8-4) eliminates such hums (www.xitel.com, $35).

8

SWITCHING BETWEEN SOUND OUTPUTS (MAC)

We covered changing sound outputs for Windows earlier; here's how you Mac users can do it.

1. Select **System Preferences** under the **Apple** menu. Click the **Sound** icon.

2. Under the **Input** and **Output** tabs, you'll see the various sound outputs listed. Click your preferred output to select it.

3. You can also change **Input** and **Output** volume levels here using the horizontal slider, and you can add **Sound Effect**.

Figure 8-4: *The Ground Loop Isolator from Xitel was designed specifically to get rid of hums that can occur when you connect your computer to your stereo. In extreme cases, it can even prevent damage.*

TIP

Most dual RCA cables peel away from each other, creating two digital coaxial cables (you'll only need one).

Computer-to-Stereo Digital Connection

If both your computer and stereo have digital connections and they're pretty close together, go with a pure digital connection between your computer and your stereo (as opposed to the analog method we just covered). This means that every 1 and 0 representing the decompressed song goes from the sound card to your speakers without being converted into analog on the way. The result: clearer sound. The most common output found on sound cards is digital coaxial (S/PDIF), which uses a single RCA cable (Figure 8-5).

Certain sound cards and external USB audio devices have a digital optical (TOSlink) output too, which transmits the same information using a laser beam sent over optical fibers. A few decades

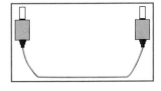

Figure 8-5: *A shielded RCA cable that's shielded from outside interference works best, but you can also use half of any old dual red-and-white RCA cable.*

QUICKSTEPS

THE DATA CD: ANOTHER COMPUTER-TO-STEREO CONNECTION

This chapter describes a number of elegant ways to put digital music on your stereo, but we'd be remiss if we didn't mention one of the simplest: burning a data CD-R filled with MP3s for playing on any CD or DVD player that supports MP3 CDs (which covers an increasing percentage of both home and portable CD and DVD players).

1. Open iTunes, and go to **Edit | Preferences | Burning**.

2. Click the button for **MP3 CD**; or, if you know that your CD or DVD player supports playlists, click **Data CD or DVD**. The former choice is more reliable, but the latter lets you burn multiple playlists onto the disc.

3. Create a playlist of the songs you want to burn onto the CD-R. Generally, you want to make the playlist 650MB or 740MB, depending on the capacity of the disc you're burning it to (iTunes shows you how big the playlist is at the bottom of the window).

4. Insert a blank CD-R.

5. Click the **Burn** button at the upper right of the iTunes window.

NOTE

To control iTunes from a room that's far away from your computer, check out the section on the AirPort Express later in this chapter. There's a remote that connects directly to that, allowing playback control (and listening) from any room in the house.

ago, this would have sounded pretty far out. Most electronics stores carry TOSlink cables in various lengths (Figure 8-6), or you can search online for *toslink cable* and turn up all sorts of options (you want a mini TOSlink cable because the larger pro version won't fit).

Figure 8-6: *Like digital coaxial cable, this digital optical cable carries the left and right channels on a single cable.*

Remote Controls for iTunes

We (barely) remember a time before televisions and stereos came with remote controls, but from what we remember, it was pretty annoying to have to walk across the room to change the channel or tweak the volume. Why, then, do so many people put up with that when it comes to playing music on their computers? The following hardware add-ons let you control iTunes wirelessly from various distances.

Logitech MediaPlay Cordless Mouse (Windows, RF)

The MediaPlay mouse from Logitech (Figure 8-7) is a wireless mouse that doubles as a remote control—such a simple concept, we're wondering why it didn't come around earlier. Pick iTunes as the software you want the mouse to work with, and it'll put **Play/Pause**, **Fast Forward**, **Rewind**, **Volume**, and **Open iTunes** right at your fingertips so you don't have to click over to iTunes when you're listening at your computer. When you're on the couch, you can use the mouse as a remote (from between 10 and 17 feet, depending on where your open USB port is and whether you use the included cable extension). The color options are gray/blue or black/red, and it costs about $50 online.

Figure 8-7:
This MediaPlay mouse is the best (and only) mouse we've seen with buttons for controlling iTunes.

Griffin Technology AirClickUSB (RF)

For longer distances, try the AirClickUSB from Griffin Technology (Figure 8-8) for Mac or Windows. It controls all the standard iTunes playback functions from distances of up to 60 feet from your computer in any direction, even penetrating through walls. The remote's tiny enough not to add clutter at home and comes with a cradle that straps to your arm, steering wheel, handlebars, or whatever when you're out and about. Griffin sells it for $40 (www.griffintechnology.com).

Keyspan Remote Control (IR)

Keyspan (www.keyspan.com) offers several infrared (IR) remote controls that work with iTunes on either Macintosh or Windows. We recommend the Keyspan Express Remote if you're looking for an IR solution, since it also works with the AirPort Express, a piece of audio networking covered later in this chapter. However, if you know you're not going to want to use the AirPort Express compatibility, consider Keyspan's other iTunes-compatible remote, the Keyspan Digital Media Remote. It's cheaper.

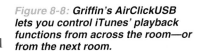

Figure 8-8: **Griffin's AirClickUSB lets you control iTunes' playback functions from across the room—or from the next room.**

CAUTION

If you have a first-generation iPod Photo (40GB or 60GB), stay away from RF remote controls, because those models can cause interference with the remote. However, that shouldn't necessarily rule out using an RF remote to control iTunes anyway, as long as you don't have your iPod Photo turned on near the remote or computer.

THE DIFFERENCE BETWEEN IR AND RF

Remote controls normally found around the home use electromagnetic signals to communicate with TVs, stereos, and similar equipment. Shorter electromagnetic waves can't get around or through things as easily as longer waves can, although in some cases they're more persistent. IR (infrared) has a shorter wavelength than RF (radio), a fact that gives each certain advantages when used as a means of remote control. Can't stand the physics anymore? Here's how it breaks down.

	PROS	CONS
RF Remote Controls	Communicate through walls, backpacks, and other obstacles.	Can interfere and suffer interference from wireless network, appliances, and the like.
IR Remote Controls	Compatible with universal remotes; less likely to suffer interference.	Can suffer interference from fluorescent lights (rare).

Multimedia Keyboard

Some keyboards sold today have buttons along the top or to the side for controlling audio playback, alongside other buttons for e-mail, favorites, and so on. We like the Microsoft Wireless Desktop Elite (Windows only, Figure 8-9) because it's wireless and has dedicated **Play/Pause**, **Stop**, **Mute**, **Volume**, **FF**, **Rewind**, and **Launch** buttons that work flawlessly with iTunes. You also get a bunch of other handy controls, such as a scroll wheel and buttons for browse back, browse forward, calculator, and more, plus an ergonomic wrist pad and an optical wireless mouse. All you need is an open USB port and about a hundred bucks (mouse included). Like all USB devices, it can be used with a desktop or a laptop.

If you don't need a wireless optical mouse (or want to spend this much money), Microsoft and other companies also offer multimedia keyboards that have buttons that can be assigned to iTunes playback functions.

*Figure 8-9: **Approximately half of this book was typed on a Microsoft Wireless Desktop Elite, controlling iTunes with its music controls for most of the way.***

TIP

Check out griffin.com's documentation that comes with the PowerMate and the "Tips & Tricks" section to learn how to program the PowerMate's click to fast forward, shuffle, and more.

Figure 8-10: *The Griffin PowerMate volume knob comes in black or aluminum color.*

Griffin PowerMate Volume Knob (USB)

We've seen this thing mocked on certain tech websites because it costs $45 and pretty much controls only volume. But oh, what a way to control volume! If you miss the heavy inertia of a volume knob on a nice home stereo, clicking a screen, mouse, or keyboard just doesn't cut it. The Griffin PowerMate (Figure 8-10) connects to any computer via an included USB cable; plop it on your desk and you can control volume for iTunes and all your other apps with a smooth, steady rotation and you can mute with a satisfying click. Plus, it has a cool blue light on the bottom.

Use Your Handheld/PDA or Phone as an iTunes Remote

Using a handheld or smartphone to control iTunes from anywhere in your house isn't as complicated as it sounds, although you'll have to install third-party software on a WiFi- or Bluetooth-enabled handheld or smartphone in order to do so, and your computer needs to have WiFi or Bluetooth, depending on which program you use. Check the sites for the following programs to find one that'll run on your handheld. You might also try searching the Web for *WiFi* [or] *Bluetooth iTunes remote control* to check for new programs.

- **Dead End Software Web Remote (Mac, Any Device with an Internet Connection and a Screen)** This app (www.deadendsw.com) turns your iTunes library into a web page that you can browse on any web-capable handheld or other web-enabled device. The web page is stored on your computer, and you connect to it using anything on your network that can see a web page—handhelds, smartphones, or other Internet-connected Macs.

- **FlexiPanel iTunes Remote (Windows, PocketPC, Bluetooth)** This simple remote app (www.flexipanel.com) is free, apparently as a demo for companies who might want to buy the hardware in bulk. That doesn't change the fact that it's free to try and keep.

- **Salling Clicker (Mac, Palm, Bluetooth)** Aside from controlling iTunes playback, the award-winning Salling Clicker software (www.salling.com) can control PowerPoint slide presentations, high-end audio programs, and more.

- **SmashCasi RemoteAmp (Windows, PocketPC, WiFi, Bluetooth)** This app (www.smashcasi.com) has lots of features: EQ, playlist editing, full search capabilities, and the ability to get to your music by folder or through iTunes.

Share Music over a Home/Office Network

Although streaming music from one computer to another on a network sounds a little complicated, iTunes makes it incredibly easy. Here's how you can listen to the music that's located on one computer from another computer on your home network (Ethernet cable or wireless; the same rules apply).

1. Install iTunes on both machines and add the music on it to the respective iTunes Libraries.

2. Go to **Edit | Preferences | Sharing** and check the boxes for **Look For Shared Music** and **Share My Music** on both machines (Figure 8-11).

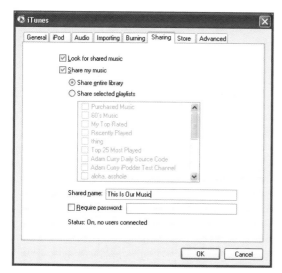

Figure 8-11: **This is the most common configuration for iTunes sharing because it shares everything and doesn't require a password.**

Figure 8-12: *If other iTunes users on your home or office network use iTunes, it's possible (and legal) for you to listen to anything in their collection; they just need to turn Sharing on.*

3. Choose a shared name; that's the name other iTunes users on the network will use to identify the computer.

4. To access music from another computer, double-click it in the upper-left area of the navigation pane on the left side of iTunes (Figure 8-12).

Use AirPort Express to Play iTunes Around Your Home

A few years ago, a multiroom audio system might have cost upward of $10,000, and many local businesses still offer home audio installation packages that cost considerably more than that. No longer; iTunes, along with an inexpensive piece of readily available hardware, can do the same thing. And because the AirPort Express (Figure 8-13) is made by Apple, it works seamlessly with iTunes.

QUICKSTEPS

USING AN OLD COMPUTER TO STREAM TO YOUR STEREO

Using principles already discussed in this chapter, you can repurpose an old desktop or laptop as a digital stereo component. It doesn't matter how slow the computer's processor is, since playing music doesn't take much computing power. However, the computer will need an Ethernet or wireless card, and its operating system needs to be at least Mac OS X 10.2.8 or Windows XP/2000—the minimum required to run iTunes.

1. If you're using a desktop, use the smallest monitor you have (an old 15-inch flat panel monitor is ideal) and a mouse—no keyboard required.

2. Position the computer near your stereo system and connect it to your Ethernet or wireless network.

3. Connect the computer to your stereo using the techniques covered at the beginning of this chapter.

4. Install iTunes and use iTunes Sharing to connect to the music on your network. You might also rip CDs to the new computer or copy music to it over the network.

5. Play music from the old computer's hard drive or other computers on your network over your stereo system.

6. Consider adding one of the iTunes remotes we mention in this chapter to your old computer (use an IR remote to integrate with your stereo's universal remote).

Figure 8-13: *If you have or want a wireless network, the AirPort Express is a great option. It puts iTunes music on any stereo in your house.*

Despite its simplicity of appearance and operation, the AirPort Express has diverse capabilities: it can act as the wireless hub for a home network; pipe iTunes to a stereo; and even output documents from anywhere on the network to a printer via USB. This versatility means you have a few different options when it comes to configuring an AirPort Express.

If you don't have WiFi already, you'll need to create a new wireless network with the AirPort Express (see the next section for instructions on that). The disadvantage of this setup is that it requires you to put the AirPort Express near your stereo, and if you want to use the AirPort Express to provide Internet access, it needs to connect to your DSL or cable modem via an Ethernet cable. We recommend buying two AirPort Expresses to make things easier (one to run the WiFi network and a second for the stereo connection and extending the network's coverage area).

However, if you already have wireless networking, you'll want the preferred option: adding the AirPort Express to an existing network. Once that's taken care of, you'll need to connect the AirPort Express to your stereo using either an analog or digital connection; you should also think about adding a remote.

Create a New Wireless Network with AirPort Express

Apple includes decent instructions with the AirPort Express, but using the AirPort Express to set up a new WiFi network boils down to the following steps.

1. Close iTunes, then plug the AirPort Express into a wall outlet near your stereo. Connect it to your stereo using either the digital or analog method discussed in this section.

2. Run the **AirPort Express Assistant** from the setup disc.

3. Choose the option for **Set Up A New AirPort Express**.

4. Choose **Create A New Wireless Network** on the first screen.

5. Select the new AirPort Express (most likely the only name on the list) and click **Next**.

6. Name your new network and your AirPort Express and click **Next**.

7. Choose your security settings. You'll need them to connect other computers to the network. We recommend 128-bit WEP for maximum compatibility or WPA if you're extremely worried about people getting onto your network. Click **Next**.

8. On the **Network Setup** page, choose whichever setting applies to you. If you're not trying to use the AirPort Express to provide Internet access for your network, choose the last option (**I Don't Want To Connect**). Click **Next**.

9. Create and verify the base station password for your AirPort Express, which you'll need if you want to change its settings. Click **Next** twice.

10. If you're still not connected to the AirPort Express, connect to it using Windows networking (double-click the **networking** icon in the task bar).

11. Start iTunes; at the lower right, you'll see a new drop-down menu; open it, and select your AirPort Express. Now you can hear iTunes coming out of your stereo wirelessly.

Add AirPort Express to an Existing Network

You can add the AirPort Express to a network created by another AirPort Express, or any other standard (802.11b/802.11g) wireless base station. If you have multiple stereos, you can even put one next to each of them.

1. Close iTunes, then plug the AirPort Express into a wall outlet near your stereo. Connect it to your stereo using either the digital or analog method discussed in this section.

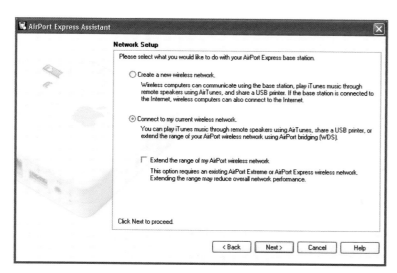

Figure 8-14: **Choose Connect To My Current Wireless Network and decide whether to extend the range of your existing network (AirPort Express and Extreme only).**

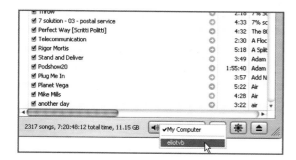

Figure 8-15: **Once everything's set up, you'll see the AirPort Express in the new drop-down menu at the lower right of iTunes. (It'll say My Computer for starters, since outputting through your own computer speakers is the default; here, my AirPort Express audio output is called "eliotvb".)**

2. Run the **AirPort Express Assistant** from the setup disc.

3. Choose the option for **Set Up A New AirPort Express** and click **Next**.

4. Pick **Connect To My Current Wireless Network** (Figure 8-14). If your main wireless base station is another AirPort Express or an AirPort Extreme and you want your wireless network to cover more area, check the box for **Extend The Range Of My AirPort Wireless Network**. Then, click Next.

5. Choose the new AirPort Express from the list, and then (you guessed it), click **Next**.

6. After the AirPort Express Assistant detects and restarts the AirPort Express, choose your wireless network and name your AirPort Express.

7. Pick and confirm the password for the AirPort Express (you can send iTunes music from other computers using this password), check the box for **Remember This Password**, and click **Next** twice.

8. Start iTunes; at the lower right, you'll see a new drop-down menu (Figure 8-15); open it, and select your AirPort Express. Now you can hear iTunes coming out of your stereo wirelessly.

AirPort-to-Stereo Analog Connection

If your stereo lacks a digital optical TOSlink input, use this option. It's quite similar to the method for connecting a sound card or USB audio device to a stereo that we covered earlier in this chapter.

1. Connect the 1/8th-inch stereo plug on one end of a Y-cable ($5 at any electronics store, as mentioned earlier in this chapter) to the analog stereo output on the AirPort Express.

2. Connect the other end, with the dual red and white RCA cables, to your stereo's **Aux In** jacks, or another open analog input (anything except for **Phono**).

3. Select the input you used in step 2 on your stereo (most likely **Aux In** or **Tape In**).

4. Assuming you've already set up the AirPort Express in iTunes (as instructed earlier in this chapter), you can now play iTunes through your stereo.

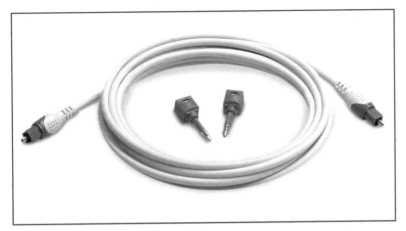

*Figure 8-16: **The Griffin XpressCable (www.griffintechnology.com, $20) isn't very long, but its white color complements the rest of your Apple stuff. Digital optical TOSlink cables from other manufacturers work, too.***

AirPort-to-Stereo Digital Connection

If your stereo has a digital optical TOSlink input, use this method for cleaner sound. Apple doesn't include any audio cables with the AirPort Express, so you'll need to buy a digital optical TOSlink cable (covered earlier in this chapter).

1. Connect one end of the digital optical TOSlink cable (Figure 8-16) to the AirPort Express.
2. Connect the other end of the TOSlink cable to your stereo's digital optical input.
3. Select the digital auxiliary input on your stereo.
4. Assuming you've already set up the AirPort Express in iTunes (earlier in this chapter), you can now play iTunes through your stereo.

CAUTION

There are several networking products available for sending music from your computer to your stereo, but (as of now) the only one that works with songs purchased from iTunes is the Apple AirPort Express.

NOTE

Xitel sells a 30-foot digital optical TOSlink cable for $10 (www.xitel.com), if you need the length.

AirPort Express Accessories

As with just about anything made by Apple, third-party manufacturers sell add-ons that can enhance the AirPort Express.

Keyspan Express Remote (IR, Mac, or Windows)

Connect this one to the USB port on the AirPort Express (Figure 8-17) and you can control iTunes from whatever room your AirPort Express is in. It controls basic playback functions and volume, but our favorite is the **Cycle** button, which shuffles either all tracks or only the tracks in the current playlist. You can find the Keyspan Express Remote at www.keyspan.com for about $60.

If you really want to connect your AirPort Express to your stereo but your stereo only has a digital coaxial input (as opposed to the digital optical TOSlink the AirPort Express outputs), you can buy a converter at some electronics stores or online for $30–$150. The M-Audio CO2 is one example ($80, www.m-audio.com), but you can find generic brands at lower prices, and since they're digital, they should sound just as good.

Figure 8-17: **The design isn't as tight as something Apple would develop, but it gets the job done nicely.**

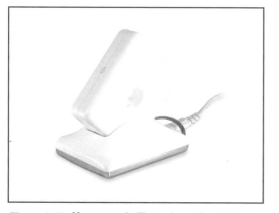

Figure 8-18: **Many people like to keep the AirPort Express tucked away, but for those who don't, Griffin's AirBase lets you display it on any horizontal surface.**

Griffin Technology AirBase AirPort Express Stand

Although plugging the AirPort Express directly into a wall works fine for most situations, the Griffin Technology AirBase desktop stand (Figure 8-18, www.griffintechnology.com, $25) can extend your wireless range, showcase the AirPort Express on a surface at a jaunty angle, or give you an extra few feet for connecting the AirPort Express to your stereo with its eight-foot cable.

At Home with the iPod

Rather than connecting iTunes to your stereo, you may prefer the simplicity of using the iPod itself as a stereo component. This requires only one wire, and if you use the docking station or a remote control with a stand, the iPod can stand at an accessible angle, whether you want to use the iPod's controls or a remote.

Apple didn't include a digital output on the iPod, so connecting the iPod to your stereo is always an analog affair, using the infamous Y-cable (refer back to Figure 8-3).

iPod Remotes for the Home

The iPod works much better as a home stereo component if you use an iPod remote with it. We recommend the Griffin AirClick (RF, www.griffintechnology .com, $40) or the Ten Technology NaviPro eX (IR, www.tentechnology.com, $50). The Griffin BlueTrip (Figure 8-19) uses Bluetooth to allow your iPod to play (and control) music on your stereo—essentially employing the iPod as both music source and remote. The Griffen BlueTrip sounds excellent and is currently available from griffentechnology.com for $150.

For more on currently available iPod remotes, see Chapter 7; we covered the difference between IR and RF earlier in this chapter. The IR or RF decision is just as important here as it is when choosing a remote for iTunes.

Apple iPod Docks

You can use a Y-cable to connect your iPod to your stereo and just leave it lying somewhere, but the iPod's smooth back means it'll slide right off if you nudge the cable by mistake. For stability, the weighted, rubber-backed dock sold by Apple is the best option. If you want to skimp on that, you can get a remote control that has a stand and take care of the remote problem that way. As always, the difference between IR and RF must be kept in mind when making a decision about a remote control.

Apple used to include a dock with some iPods, but these days you'll most likely have to pick one up as an accessory. iPod sells three different docks for each model (iPod, iPod Mini, and iPod Photo, www.apple.com, $39) that allow you to connect to your stereo and power supply instantly by dropping the iPod into the dock.

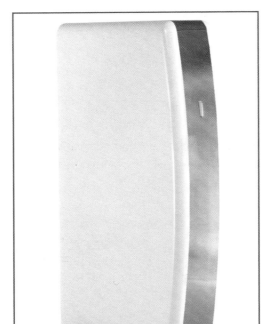

Figure 8-19: *This could be the killer app for iPod-stereo connection, with an estimated 30-foot range using a Bluetooth adapter for the iPod and this stylish stereo component.*

NOTE

iPod docks come with connectors for both Firewire and USB.

TIP

If you have lots of digital images on your iPod Photo, it really is worth connecting both audio and video to your entertainment system. Watching slideshows of photo albums as audio plays from your iPod is great, whether you're home alone or throwing a party.

You can get a dock for the Shuffle, but it's for USB rather than stereo connection. (Maybe Apple or some third-party manufacturer will make an iPod Shuffle home stereo dock someday.)

APPLE iPOD DOCK

Designed for any "regular" dockable iPod (as opposed to the Mini or Photo), this dock provides connections for power and the stereo via a Y-cable. There's no digital connection option, but the regular analog cables usually sound fine. It holds every capacity of dockable iPod available and holds the iPod at a nice angle on the top of any stereo.

APPLE iPOD MINI DOCK

With a narrower slot for the more svelte iPod Mini, this dock gives you everything the larger iPod Dock does: 1/8th-inch analog stereo output and the power input. Your iPod Mini will be on display and connecting it to power and your stereo will be a snap.

APPLE iPOD PHOTO DOCK

The iPod Photo Dock is different in that it helps your iPod Photo get along even better with your television and stereo, adding an S-video output for sending slideshow video to your television with added clarity. You can also still use the triple-RCA cable included with the iPod Photo to send audio and video to your stereo and television.

XITEL iPOD HIFI-LINK

Apple's docks are handy, but if you want something with a bit more oomph, Xitel's iPod HiFi-Link is the way to go. Drop your dockable iPod, iPod Photo, or iPod Mini into the iPod HiFi-Link and you'll be connected to your stereo more cleanly, since it uses two individual RCA cables rather than the Y-cable Apple's dock uses. But that's a minor detail compared with the fact that Xitel also throws in a remote control for controlling volume and playback functions, as well as a knob for adding varying degrees of TruBass. This signal processor adds bass that gets lost when you compress your music into MP3 or AAC. At $79, the Xitel iPod HiFi-Link costs about twice as much as Apple's dock, but if you plan on using your iPod with a stereo or set of powered speakers quite a bit, it's worth it.

BELKIN TUNESTAGE

This innovating system lets you use your iPod like a remote control for your stereo. Well, not exactly, but that's what the Belkin TuneStage ($180, belkin.com) feels like. Snap the Bluetooth transmitter onto the top of your iPod, and control playback as you would normally—except instead of coming out of headphones, the music will come out of your stereo. The system works up to 33 feet and can see through walls.

How To...

Chapter 9
Tapping into Advanced Audio Sources

As a sophisticated piece of technology, the iPod is a tool that lets you access more music from a much wider variety of sources than similar devices in the past. This chapter is about helping you to find those sources and make the best use of them.

Why Finding Music Has Changed

Imagine if there were just one telephone in the world: with no other unit to connect with, it would not be a very useful tool. But when there are millions of others, suddenly it's so handy that—if you're like us—you must have one with you at all times. Similarly, the iPod is best viewed as one node in a vast network. The reason it (along with other digital music players) is so powerful is because it draws from the strength of a network.

That network has grown. Despite the dire reports about the health of the music industry, the sheer amount of audio—both musical and nonmusical—has grown enormously over the last decade, as most barriers to entry fall. It shows no signs of letting up. The iPod, hooked into your networked computer, is able to interface and play most of those sound files distributed, and you benefit by access to the richest sonic banquet yet served on this planet. Where tune-hungry teenagers of the past had to work to find anything interesting, you, lucky inhabitant of the 21st century, are spoiled by choices.

The New Music Business

The exciting thing about the iPod, and digital music in general, is that it encourages people to rethink past business practices and dream up new plans to take advantage of the Net's ability to reach many more people in places much farther away than is possible with radio or CDs. The expense of marketing physical goods—networks of shipping, warehousing, and distribution—was a strong factor in limiting the range of available music. The physical marketplace worked very well for its time, but the reach of digital networks has already surpassed it. It has also opened the pathway for dedicated amateurs to publish, network, and become an interesting species of musical archivists and promoters through the use of MP3 blogs and podcasts.

The outcome of this broadening of publishing and marketing options is very much in play, and everyone is still trying to wrap their heads around what it will mean. One effect is that releasing sounds that appeal to a smaller niche is more doable. Without needing to send a physical object to faraway stores to find a buyer, publishing works that appeal to, say, five hundred people now makes more economic sense, empowering the ability of like-minded enthusiasts to spread the word about their favorite sounds.

Rework What You've Got

The other cool thing about being part of a powerful information-processing machine (your computer) is that you can reformat other types of media to play

QUICKSTEPS

USING MP3 BLOGS FOR MUSIC DISCOVERY

1. Start your web browser.

2. Open an MP3 blog site. (There is a short list of popular sites in the next section.)

3. Read what the blogger says about a given piece of music and, if you find something interesting, download it (the link to the file should be fairly obvious) and give it a listen. To download, right-click the filename and save.

4. You might want to keep a separate folder for music you discover using MP3 blogs because chances are you won't like everything. A separate folder makes it easy to throw away music that doesn't interest you.

TIP

Starting your own blog is beyond the scope of this book, but if you're interested in blogging, there's no reason you can't try writing your own. Go to the sites of blogging software companies like Wordpress.org, Blogger.com, or SixApart.com to get started.

on the iPod. Albums, cassette tapes, even 8-track tapes are all fair game for a revitalized and newly portable library of yours.

MP3 Blogs

We bet you've heard of blogs. Very few Net applications have created such a stir as this convenient packaging of tools for self-publishing. Suddenly everyone who has something to say can say it to an audience limited only by their ability to hold interest. Journalism can suddenly be fact-checked and held accountable. And with millions of self-publishers out there, it really is impossible to keep up with all your reading.

MP3 blogs are an interesting twist on the concept of people writing about what they're listening to, and in many cases they post files of those songs so that others can hear them too (Figure 9-1). The whole notion of word-of-mouth has been updated. However, because the record industry thrives on publicity for its bands but doesn't like freely distributed MP3s, the whole idea of MP3 blogs sort of has the industry scratching its collective head. Is it good for building buzz? What's the use of buzz if everyone already has a copy of the hit song? The questions fly around but in the meantime, the action continues to swell, and as a tool for discovery it's hard to miss the appeal.

Get Started with MP3 Blogs

Here's a short list of some MP3 blogs to get you started:

- **www.fluxblog.org**   This blog has been around a long time and sets a good standard of introducing people to interesting stuff.

- **www.mp3blogs.org**   The MP3Blogs Aggregator, this site pulls together a diverse group of MP3 blogs for your perusal.

- **Monkey Filter**   Yes, it's a big link (wiki.monkeyfilter.com/index.php?title=MP3_Blog_Listing), but it's an even bigger list of MP3 blogs, divided into categories (Figure 9-2).

- **soul-sides.com**   A great collector of vintage and current soul, with rare tracks posted for ten days. For lovers of soul, this site alone justifies the whole Internet.

Figure 9-1: *Music blogs like Tofu Hut are changing the way listeners discover music.*

- **music.for-robots.com** An indie-music blog that's turned into a phenomenon, with CDs of favorites and shows they've curated at New York's Knitting Factory.

- **saidthegramophone.com** "If I were Swedish, created in 1997, and a piece of music and not a person, I might be this song. But if I were, I would sing like a girl, and I don't want to do that." With free-flowing introductions like that and an interesting selection of songs, this blog is great for discovering new indie pop.

- **swedesplease.blogspot.com** Speaking of Sweden, did you know that Swedish music (along with Nordic music in general) is in the midst of a kind of peak moment? See for yourself at this tribute blog to new Swedish bands.

- **tofuhut.blogspot.com** One of the most active and fun MP3 blogs, often with random kooky videos for your amusement, as well as a great eclectic mix of cool music.

Some of what's linked to download on MP3 blogs falls into legally shady territory. You should read up on what is and isn't legal before you jump in. Though learning about this stuff is admittedly tricky business, we can recommend the Internet rights advocacy group the Electronic Frontier Foundation as a good place to start your education about file sharing (www.eff.org/share/).

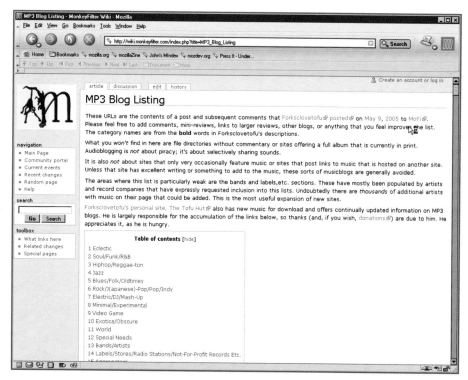

Figure 9-2: **Monkey Filter has a great number of diverse music blogs listed.**

Enter the Podcast

Sometimes several technologies rise concurrently, feeding on each other's strengths to make each other powerful. The ascent of RSS (Real Simple Syndication) went hand-in-hand with blogging. With so many different voices publishing every day (Figure 9-3), how could anyone keep up with their favorite blogs, let alone a well-rounded mix of wider views? The answer came with the RSS feeds, basically stripped down versions of blog postings that were published in a format that RSS reading programs could pick up and pull together for each user. Sort of like a user-assembled newspaper. Many bloggers swear by them.

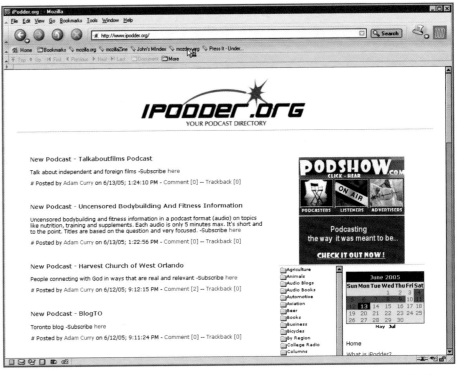

Figure 9-3: *The iPodder homepage is a directory of diverse topics and a window into the many faces of modern life.*

 **NOTE**

If you'd like to learn more about creating your own podcast, see Chapter 10.

The same principle was applied to the idea of distributing audio programming. With the strong audio production capabilities inherent in even the cheapest personal computers these days, many motivated users have started creating their own radio shows. But how to keep up? The answer is audio programming mixed with RSS tracking—and the podcast is born.

Podcasts work by syndicating themselves—that is, the podcast audio file is published however irregularly, and listeners must run a program to listen to them; that program checks to see if a new subscribed podcast is published. If so, it downloads it and prepares it for syncing to iPods or for play on the computer.

How to Use Podcasts

In the recent past, if you wanted to get into the world of podcasting you had to install a separate program such as iPodder. Now with the inclusion of podcast capabilities in the latest iTunes, jumping in with the Apple standard is about the easiest way to get audio into iTunes and your iPod.

Of course, if you'd like a little more power and flexibility than iTunes provides, you'll want to use an external program. We like iPodder (Figure 9-4) because it's reliable and works for both Mac and Windows machines. There are plenty of others, but because the technology is fairly simple, it's mainly a case of picking one with an appealing design for you.

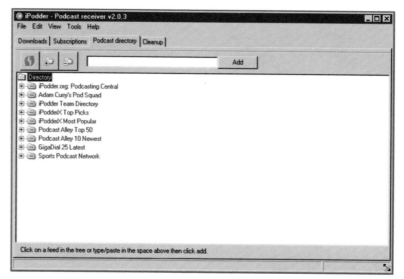

*Figure 9-4: **iPodder is one of several good podcasting programs.***

Audio Books

As you've seen with the podcast, the iPod is not just for music. In fact, there is a thriving trade in audio books that has resulted from the spread of digital music players. Many people who bought an iPod for the sake of playing music find that its real benefit is the ability to listen to full-length books during their commute. This spoken medium returns literature to its storytelling roots.

AUDIBLE.COM

Apple has always seemed to have a good relationship with producer Audible.com, and the result is that iPod users can pick from a vast library of spoken books, magazines, and instructional guides, all gathered in one place (Figure 9-5).

*Figure 9-5: **Audible.com is full of good listening—but you have to sign up first to see what it really offers.***

Our main beef with Audible is that you have to join up before you can see what is actually available and how much it costs. Sure there are examples of books, but why not open the whole store for a look? The other beef is that it uses its own proprietary Audible Audio format. Why introduce more confusion into the market?

On the other hand, the selection is good, and it has enough devoted listeners to be worth at least a try.

OTHER AUDIO BOOKSTORES

Pay Per Listen (payperlisten.com) and AudioBooksOnline (www.audiobooks online.com) are two other services that are more straightforward, if not as comprehensive. Their selections aren't as big as Audible's, but at least you are able to see what's offered before you sign up for anything—and they use the good old MP3 format.

CD BOOK SOLUTIONS

Publishers are still selling a lot of audio books in the CD format, which as you know, is easy to import into iTunes as a digital file to be played by your computer or iPod. Amazon and Barnes & Noble have a load of these online (Figure 9-6), as do many other booksellers. Since the audio quality is less important than with music, you can experiment with lower fidelity settings to fit a lot more book on your iPod.

EVEN MORE LEARNING

Want to be really erudite? The Teaching Company (www.teach12.com) sells CDs of college lectures from very engaging professors. It might seem square, but actually the innate joy of learning is very strong, and these kinds of courses can be really fun as well as enriching. The subject range is vast and includes introductions to jazz and classical music, the history of the English language, particle physics, and the philosophy of religion. And listen up, kids: It's also a great way to convince your parents that the iPod is an educational tool.

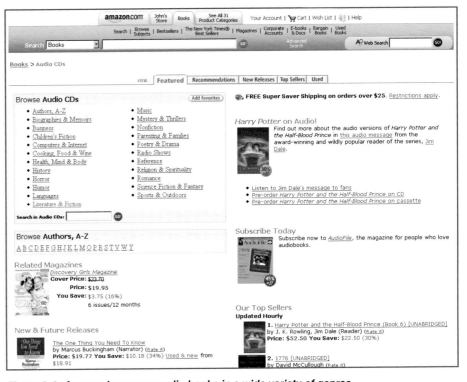

NOTE

If you're a frequent user of audio books, you're probably wondering if there's a better way to keep track of where you are in each book. There is. Markable by iPodSoft (www.ipodsoft.com) lets you mark your place in audio books (or lectures and podcasts) with ease.

QUICKFACTS

MAKING IT TALK

Mac users have an extra bonus when it comes to audio: Zapptek iSpeak. This program lets you input text and output spoken word using the Macintosh's built-in speech engine. While it's not nearly as easy on the ears (or the imagination) as a human speaker, there is something cool about being read stories by your computer. Are you there, Hal?

Figure 9-6: *Amazon has many audio books in a wide variety of genres.*

To listen to these on your iPod, just order regular CDs and import them to iTunes at a lower bit rate than you'd use for high-quality music.

Digital Labels and Digital Music Stores

It's quite possible that the music on iTunes alone is enough to keep you happily in tunage for the rest of your life. It's that comprehensive. But for several reasons it's worth checking out what other ways there are to acquire music.

There's a growing consensus that online is where it's at, and many upstart music labels and distributors are taking the leap into digital-only territory.

You might care about supporting diverse sources in the marketplace, buying music from lesser-known artists, or using song files that are encoded without the hampering effects of digital rights management. All of those are worthy reasons to use these other sources, and the fact that some offer music cheaper can sweeten the deal.

The one drawback to diverging from the familiarity of iTunes is just that: you've lost your bearings somewhat and may need to learn some different ways of downloading and paying. For many, this kind of freedom is a good thing— new discoveries must be within reach. For others it's just a nuisance. Which type are you?

Here's a quick roster of some of the most popular and interesting digital stores and labels that offer music compatible with the iPod.

BEATPORT.COM

Created in partnership with music software company Native Instruments, this DJ-oriented site lets you download some top grooves in the highest fidelity (Figure 9-7). To emphasize the professional nature of the sites, song files are offered in large-size 320K MP3, WAV, or MP4 formats. If you want to stay on top of the latest music, especially if you have a finicky audience to please, this is a great way to do it.

NUGS.NET

One little-known historical factoid is that the tape-trading world of the Grateful Dead and its followers, as well as the audio-technical knowledge of that scene's tinkers, has provided a lot of the fertile ground from which the world of online music rose. Continuing the tradition, Nugs.net offers albums and full shows from a jam-band heavy roster of songsmiths like Widespread Panic, Galactica, and String Cheese Incident, in either MP3 or the FLAC lossless codec.

*Figure 9-7: **Beatport has a lot of music for serious DJs—and those who wish they were.***

BLEEP (BLEEP.COM)

Electronic music label Warp Records has been cutting edge with the sound
of its artists, so it's only natural that it would get in on the act with its own
online shop. From the website, you can buy MP3s, and if you're interested in
announcing your music to the world, you can also purchase higher-priced ring
tones. For fans of Warp bands like Aphex Twin and Autechre this is the only
authorized place to find their music online.

EMUSIC (EMUSIC.COM)

While many of the recent big-name subscription services like Rhapsody, Napster, and Yahoo are incompatible with the iPod because it sticks with the venerable MP3 format and shuns digital rights management, online stalwart Emusic is usable by iPod owners. It offers a lot of great music, but as with Audible, it requires you to sign up to see the full depth of the catalog.

Find Bootleg Traders

In the old days, some fans would sneak tape recorders into concerts and leave with permanent records of their favorites, eventually trading tapes with other fans. Instead of trying to end this practice, bands like the Grateful Dead latched on to it and used those legions of tape traders as an army of marketers encouraging others to see (and pay for) each show in person.

Now that music culture has made its way into the digital age, many bands, especially those of the Dead-like "jam band" mold, freely encourage their fans to trade digital recordings of their performances. You can tap into this network and learn about bands you might not have heard of, as well as find some interesting recordings of old favorites.

Check out www.archive.org/audio/etree.php for easy-to-find downloads, or go to Tape Trader (www.tapetrader.com/) for a bulletin board that facilitates trading of both song files and physical copies.

Note that many serious online traders are archivists at heart and want only the best, so they often use the FLAC format, a lossless codec. To use those on your iPod, you'll need a converter program. There are many shareware and pay programs that do this. Just do a search on <u>FLAC MP3 Converter</u> at Google or Download.com.

NOTE

Like many other things in the file sharing world, bootleg trading is a gray area. Many bands give their explicit permission to tapers and traders to operate freely. Others are hesitant to give away something whose quality they can't control. If you're concerned about this, your best bet is to stick with the larger sites, which usually do a fair degree of policing to keep out any infringers.

Find Early Recordings

A lot of great music was recorded in the early part of last century and released as 78-rpm records. Because that music mostly falls under public domain now, there are sites dedicated to preserving, digitizing, and distributing them. Check out the Internet Archive's collection of hundreds of artists at www.archive.org/audio/collection.php?collection=78rpm.

The American Library of Congress also has a weighty collection of music as well as interviews and narratives that stretch from last century to this one. See memory.loc.gov/ammem/browse/ListSome.php?format=Sound+Recording.

For north-of-the-border music history, check out the Virtual Gramophone at www.collectionscanada.ca/gramophone/index-e.html.

Digital Radio

Even if you don't purchase any music whatsoever, with iTunes and an Internet connection you can tune into a world of sound. iTunes comes equipped with the ability to stream audio, which works just like downloading but nothing is saved. The music plays and then, unless you've hooked up special recording software, it's gone forever.

Did you have a favorite college radio station? There's a chance that it's putting out a stream of music that you can listen to. Are you far from your home country? Take a look around and you'll probably find that someone, somewhere is broadcasting the music you love.

The iTunes Radio capability is an easy fit with the rest of the program's options and offers a huge variety of channels—certainly a lot more than what's being broadcast on your standard radio these days (Figure 9-8).

NOTE

The Bit Rate column shown in Figure 9-8 tells you at what rate of fidelity the station is broadcasting. The higher the number, the better the sound (and the faster the Internet connection you'll need to receive it).

*Figure 9-8: **The iTunes Radio lineup, drawn from around the world, offers an impressive roster of music (and a few news choices).***

Find Even More Stations!

Just because a streaming station isn't in the official Apple roster doesn't mean that iTunes won't play it. You can easily pick from a huge variety of stations supported by Shoutcast (Figure 9-9) and Live365. You can add them to your musical library or, more conveniently, you can create a playlist for streaming radio and add the stations you want. Note: if you listen to Live365, you'll hear ads.

QUICKSTEPS

ADDING ADDITIONAL RADIO STATIONS

1. Create a new playlist and call it something like MoreRadio.

2. Use your web browser and go to www.shoutcast .com or www.live365.com. Use the site's navigation to find a station that interests you.

3. Click the **Play** button, which should bring up a dialog box asking what you want to do with the file (which bears the extension .pls). Choose to save the file in a new folder somewhere (it's up to you exactly where). It's a good idea to rename the file by what it contains, such as "metal.pls" or something similar, so that you can keep track of different stations.

4. Open your empty new playlist and drag the .pls file. At first it won't look like much, but once you double-click it, the **song name** category should fill with more detail.

5. You can add as many of these stations as you'd like. Just remember that even though it's a playlist, you can't expect to listen sequentially (because the stations, unlike songs, don't end). Since most of these streams stay up continuously, you'll have to manually click another if you want to change channels.

Figure 9-9: *Shoutcast, like Live365, offers even more radio variety that can be used, with just a little effort, in iTunes.*

TURNING VINYL INTO MP3S

Keep in mind these same techniques can be used for recording from cassette tapes, radio, 8-track tape, or just about anything else. For some formats, you'll want to process them a little more to make them sound a little less hissy.

1. Download and install your audio program. Get it up and running according to its maker's directions.

2. Connect the cable from your stereo to your computer. Choose **Line-In** as the audio source. (Some soundcards have several different lines in. If you're not getting any sound in the next step, make sure you've picked the right one.)

3. Choose **Preferences In** and pick the quality you want to record in. **44100 Hz** is good. (That's CD quality.) Be sure that inputs are set to **Stereo**.

4. Pick a loud song and start playing the record. Then start recording; this is just to get an idea of the sound level. You should see waveforms forming like a mountain range, but these should never go into peak red territory. If they do, adjust the volume down.

5. Once you have a good idea of the sound levels, start recording the album. You can split up the songs later or record them one-by-one now.

Continued . . .

NOTE

If you don't have a stereo setup but you do have a turntable, the Griffin Turntable Connection Cable has what you need, complete with grounding capabilities to remove any hum.

Record from Old Vinyl

Previously we told you how to turn your collection of CDs into files that were playable on your computer and iPod. But maybe your collection goes back much further than last year's hits. Maybe it goes all the way back to the Summer of Love in 1967, or before. In that case, you've probably got a lot of old records. In fact vinyl has a lot going for it, and many audiophiles still prefer its warmth and fidelity. But they can't listen to those LPs on their morning commute.

Though making digital duplicates of LPs is a lot more complicated than the pop-in-and-rip ease of CDs, it's not that difficult, and the reward—especially if you've got a treasured collection—is well worth it.

Here's what you'll need to get started:

- At least one vinyl record and a turntable connected to a stereo receiver.

- A cable to run from your stereo to the sound input on your computer. This usually calls for an RCA-to-miniplug cable, but if your computer supports RCA jacks, get RCA to RCA.

- An audio editing program like Audacity (audacity.sourceforge.net), Goldwave (goldwave .com), or Sound Forge. The first two are shareware so you can experiment freely.

- A program called dBPowerAmp is very helpful with renaming and editing song information. Not strictly necessary.

Record from Your Stereo to Your Computer

Although iTunes itself doesn't record, you can use a connection similar to the one you use for tapes to record from your stereo (playing tapes, vinyl, AM, FM, etc.) onto your computer, and then import those recordings into iTunes. After that, you'll be able to play them as you do any other file on your iPod, as well as at home using iTunes.

6. Once you've recorded the songs, take a listen and make sure they sound good. You can use the **Normalize** effect or processing to raise the sound to normal levels without peaking. Other processing you might want to consider is noise removal or pop/hiss removal, depending on what's offered by your software.

7. If you're hoping to also burn CDs from these songs, do it now, before you convert them into MP3s. After conversion they will lose some sound quality. To burn to CD, you can use iTunes, the software that came with your burner, or whatever audio editing program you're using now. (Sound Forge's is very sophisticated.)

8. If you want the album separated into songs, you can use the cursor in the program to isolate each song's audio and then cut and paste it into a new file, just like you might do with text or pictures. Or, if you want a solid album, you can join the recordings of both sides into one big file.

9. Once you've got your tracks the way you want them, you can convert them to MP3s. For most programs it's a simple matter of selecting **Save As** or **Export As MP3**.

10. Download and install dBPowerAmp and right-click files to label them so that they're not all called Untitled or Track 1. That way, the proper info will show up in iTunes and on your iPod. (You can also import these songs into iTunes and change the info there, but it's too easy to lose track of the songs in iTunes when they're untitled.)

Other Ways to Enter the iTunes Music Store

While iTunes integrates the Music Store very convincingly, this isn't the only way to buy tunes from Apple. There are other ways to enter into the vast collection than just a searching for stuff you already know about. After all, music has traditionally been shared by word-of-mouth and community recommendations. As it moves into the digital world, this aspect is not being left behind—on the contrary, it is quickly becoming supercharged by the power of the Internet's ability to connect people.

On the iTunes store itself, celebrity playlists (some of which are on the front page) can be a fun way to see into the tastes of your favorite artists and find the music that inspires them. In fact, finding a connection to an artist you hadn't really considered listening to is a good way to develop an appreciation for the artist's work.

Moving just outside of the Apple universe, MP3.com (which both authors of this book have worked on) is an outside, unbiased site designed to let music buyers comparison shop for the music they like. Because it includes up-to-date information about iTunes' offerings combined with professional music criticism and passionate groups of fans, it's a good way to see the music you like in a larger context (Figure 9-10).

Find Music on MP3.com

It's very easy to look for music on MP3.com. The advantage to it is that you're in a place where no one is trying to sell you anything (aside from the site advertising, of course). Or rather, if someone is trying to sell you an artist it's because that person is a fan of the artist's work. Bringing together fans, professional writers, and all the data from most major (and some minor) music services offers a comprehensive community for online music.

Figure 9-10: **MP3.com combines listings of music available from iTunes and others with communities of music fans.**

Though there are many other features of the site, here's a quick way to get started finding music from a band you like:

1. Go to MP3.com.

2. Enter a search term for **Artist**, **Album**, or **Song**, and check whichever you have chosen.

3. You'll either see a screen of results for what you searched on, or be taken directly to an artist's page. If you get a page of results, click whichever is closest to what you're looking for.

4. If you go to an artist's page, you can usually read all about their history, or you can go directly to their discography.

5. From the discography, you can drill down further to read album reviews and see if particular tracks are available for download from the group of music services that MP3.com monitors (including iTunes). If a song says "Available" you can click it and see all of the services that offer it for download and streaming.

6. If iTunes is listed, click the **iTunes logo** under the **Get It** column and the iTunes program should automatically launch with the song loaded and ready to purchase.

7. Note that most of the other big-name services that are listed on MP3.com are not officially compatible with iTunes, so unless you see a song offered by Emusic or smaller services that use MP3, you probably want to stick with iTunes.

Chapter 10

Becoming an iPod Jedi (the Next Level)

If you've completed everything in the previous chapters, you're already a Jedi with the iPod (we have to say it: "JediPod"—sorry). Just don't let too many people know how much you know; otherwise, the next time you go to a party, you could find yourself cornered by some clueless type asking you why they can't upload their iPod songs to their friend's computer using iTunes.

In this chapter, we'll cover advanced techniques and add-ons for iTunes and iPod alike, starting with one of the most asked-for bits of advice: how to preserve, and eventually replace, the iPod's internal battery.

Replace the Batteries

The battery on the iPod Shuffle's not likely to need replacing, even after several years of heavy use. But iPods with hard drives in them (Mini, iPod, iPod Photo) occasionally need their batteries replaced. You can have someone else do it, or take it on yourself.

Get Your iPod's Battery Replaced

If you don't mind boxing up your iPod and sending it off to be fixed, the best deals in battery replacement are online, whether you're looking for someone to supply and replace the battery or you just need the goods so you can do it yourself. However, if you live near an Apple store or Apple repair service center, you can often get a quick turnaround without paying overnight shipping fees.

LOCAL SHOPS

You might have an Apple store nearby (check here: www.apple.com/retail). Take your receipt if you have it, as well as any relevant warranty information you might have. Even if you lack all paperwork, Apple can repair or replace your iPod (prices vary).

DISCOUNT BATTERY REPLACEMENT SERVICES

A quick search of the Web will turn up several more options, whether you're looking for home replacement kits or a full service job. Just be careful not to fall for a scam and send someone a free iPod. In addition, you should always try to find out what sort of policy a potential repair service has in terms of guaranteeing results. In the unfortunate event that they send you a refurbished iPod with a hard drive that's on its last legs, it'd be nice to know that they'd make good on replacing it.

APPLE'S REPAIR SERVICE

Apple will replace any iPod's battery for $99 (plus $7 shipping), no questions asked. For this reason, you might want to stick with Apple for repairs. See

QUICKFACTS

GIVING YOUR iPOD A COLOR-TINTED SCREEN

Replacing your battery is one thing, but to take things to the next level, box up your iPod and send it to iPodMods to have a new color screen installed. Now that so many people have iPods, this could be a clever way to have yours stand out.

- Most orders come back to the customer 7–10 days after they're received, and as of the time of this writing, the company had a "100 percent satisfaction guaranteed" policy.

- It doesn't take a genius to realize that iPodMods can't replace the screen on the iPod Shuffle, because it doesn't have one. As for the iPod Photo, it already has a much better color screen than the ones they put on the black-and-white iPod 1G, 2G, 3G, 4G, and Mini.

- The replacement screen is a monochromatic color, so that it will glow with an intense hue of red, blue, green, or yellow.

- iPodMods claims that your battery performance will be the same or even better than it was with the standard screen installed.

www.apple.com/support for more on "Out-of-Warranty" battery replacement. But remember: Apple might not send back the same hard drive, so make sure everything on your iPod is stored on your computer as well.

You can also go to http://store.apple.com and look for the **AppleCare Protection Plan** for iPod. For $59, you can extend the normal one-year warranty to two years. Some users report cracked screens, hard drives damaged by bad luck, and issues with the headphone jack. It could be worth it for some users.

iPODMODS.COM

This site charges $20 to diagnose your iPod problems and does replace batteries, but the company's real emphasis is on selling iPod parts for those who wish to repair their iPods themselves. Aside from taking care of the labor on your iPod's batteries, however, iPodMods also offers a unique color screen replacement program (see QuickFacts sidebar).

iPODRESQ

You can find cheaper prices at iPodResQ ($79, last time we checked). Team up with a friend to take advantage of their "Dual Pack" battery replacement offer, which costs $120 for two iPods (iPod 1G–4G, iPod Mini, and/or iPod Photo).

Do-It-Yourself Battery Replacement

If you're the type to do it yourself, replacing the iPod's battery is a possibility. We advise against it unless you're prepared to take a chance of causing further damage to ports, jacks, or even the Hold switch. It could cost a maximum of $250 to get Apple or someone else to repair a damaged iPod (aside from battery repairs, which are a special case at $99, no questions asked). That's why it's generally a better idea to pay someone else to replace the battery and assume that risk.

If you want to save money and attempt the DIY battery replacement on your lonesome, iPodResQ sells kits for the 1G–3G iPods for $30 plus shipping. Or, if you're not sure what's wrong with it, they'll also diagnose other iPod problems

If you have a color inkjet printer and want to customize your 4G iPod with some truly zany designs, search the Web or HP.com for HP Printable Tattoos for Apple iPod. They work with any inkjet printer; $15 gets you ten sheets for the fourth-generation iPod only. Unlike real tattoos, these come off by themselves in about a month, at which point you can either revert to the original look or try a new tattoo design.

for $29 and give a repair quote (shipping and "iBox" shipping box included). If you want to do it yourself at your own risk (DIYOR), the basic theory is that you pry the metal backing off of the iPod (or, in the case of the Mini, wedge apart the metal case and pop the two glued halves apart), disconnect any ports that are in the way, put in a replacement battery (available online for $29 and up), reconnect the ports, and pop the case back together again. More detailed directions are also easily found online.

iMix Publishing

Hundreds, perhaps even thousands, of articles have been written about how the playlist is the new album. There's a certain degree of truth in that these days, since it's definitely a lot easier for people to arrange music the way mix tape enthusiasts used to, without doing all the legwork. Online playlist sharing has been hampered in the past by legal issues, but iTunes remedies this problem to a certain extent. You can publish iMixes to a public area in iTunes where other users can hear 30-second samples of the songs they don't already own and buy the songs they like, or maybe even the whole playlist. (If you're so inclined, you can even register to make money as an iTunes affiliate if you generate enough sales; we'll show you how in a bit.)

Share an iMix with the World

Publishing an iMix is easy, and all the action takes place right within iTunes.

1. Create a playlist for publication of up to 250 songs.

2. Click the little **arrow** to the right of the new playlist (Figure 10-1).

3. Click the **Create** button in the warning window that pops up telling you that it's going to send your song information to the Internet. iTunes will only publish songs it can identify in the iTunes Music Store. (It's legal to own MP3s of your music, by the way, in case you're paranoid about sending evidence of that ownership over the Internet.)

4. If you're not already signed in to iTunes, you'll need to do so now (Figure 10-2).

5. Fill out a title and description (Figure 10-3); when people listen to your iMix, they'll see both displayed within their iTunes window.

Figure 10-1: Who knows, maybe your skills as a tastemaker will gain you a reputation on iTunes; if not, at least you can share music samples with friends.

You can't publish an iMix that contains songs that iTunes cannot find in the iTunes Music Store. This causes problems with any songs that either aren't licensed for sale on iTunes or are improperly titled, whether you ripped them from CDs or got them from some other source.

Figure 10-2: *If you forgot your password, Apple can e-mail it to you.*

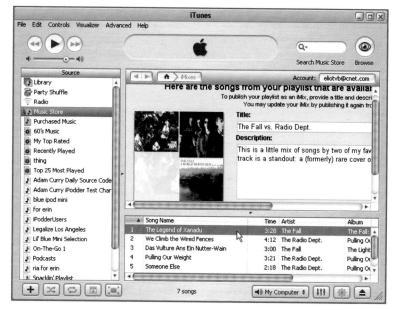

Figure 10-3: *Now the world will know about the unlikely cover of "The Legend of Xanadu" by the British band, The Fall.*

6. That's it; now when you make an iMix and share it, recipients will have to pay to hear more than a 30-second sample, unless they already own the songs on the playlist. To send out the link, click the **Tell A Friend** button (Figure 10-4).

7. Other iTunes users will be able to rate your iMix, driving it higher or lower in the ratings. Apple will save your iMix for one year.

You could even produce your own podcast in which you interview an artist or a fan and then use the iTunes affiliate program to collect a commission if your listeners end up buying music as a result. We covered subscribing to podcasts back in Chapter 9; we cover creating them later on in this chapter.

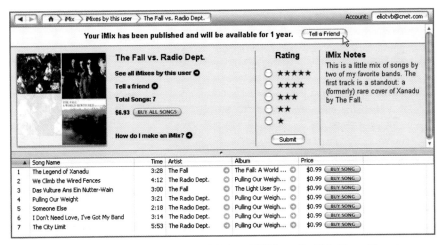

Figure 10-4: *To see all of your iMixes, click See All iMixes By This User. The stars are what listeners will use to rate your mix.*

Figure 10-5: *Here's how you get the URL for the iMix you just made.*

8. To get the URL for your iMix, right-click the album art on the upper left and select **Copy iTunes Music Store URL** when it pops up (Figure 10-5).

Make Money from iTunes

Now that you've knocked that one off, let's move on to something that might seem unnecessarily capitalistic; this is, after all, just about the music, is it not? But the Internet has always promised music fans new ways to interact with music, and that extends to influencing other fans as a tastemaker. In a sense, using your iMixes to make money for Apple and maybe even yourself is a way for you to take on two roles that exist at major labels: the A&R person (the role you assume when finding bands and picking their best songs for your iMixes) and the marketing person (in which capacity you promote your iMixes using e-mail, blogs, podcasts, instant messaging, and sheer ingenuity). iTunes' affiliate program is yet another facet of the digital music revolution that is finally coming to pass, in that it short-circuits some of the old mechanisms and democratizes taste-making and traditional promotion.

TIP

Include iMixes in your e-mail and bulletin board signatures to increase sales.

Become an iTunes Affiliate

One of the more popular sales techniques used by large-commerce websites these days is paying third parties to generate leads in an affiliate program. These work sort of like a digital Amway: affiliates get paid for influencing others to buy the songs they recommend. Amazon does this; anyone can set up a web store and send sales traffic to their site in order to get paid a percentage of resulting sales (assuming the sales reach a certain volume).

Apple's iTunes Music Store has its own take on the affiliate program based around the iMix. When you create an iMix, you get a link that any iTunes user can click to bring up the same list in an iTunes Music Store window. If you have a website or blog, use the URLs you created in step 8 of the tutorial on creating an iMix. When someone buys the songs on that list after clicking them from the link you sent or posted, 5 percent of the sale goes to your account. People can click over from any of your iMixes to a list of all of your iMixes, so if you're serious about making money as a tastemaker, don't include any duds, even though you might feel pressure to churn out a whole slew of iMixes.

To sign up as an iTunes affiliate, go to www.apple.com/itunes/affiliates/.

The rules for being an affiliate and the signup procedure are subject to change, so we haven't included them here, but you'll need your social security number, address, phone number, and some other information.

Move Your iTunes Library

iTunes lets you keep your songs on up to five computers, which might seem like a lot until you factor in upgrades. If you have two computers at home, one at school or work, and a laptop, you're only one away from the limit. Likewise, if you only have one computer but upgrade every four years or so, you'll run out of authorized computers long before you feel like losing a collection of songs you paid good money for. That's why deauthorizing iTunes on a computer is

NOTE

You can transfer songs to a new computer without deauthorizing the old one. This is a great way to set up your library and playlists on a second computer at school, home, or your room at a friend's house.

CAUTION

Make sure to deauthorize a computer before uninstalling iTunes! Otherwise, you'll have to deauthorize the account by deauthorizing all accounts in the last year by going to www.apple.com/support/itunes/authorization.html. If that fails, try iTunes technical support.

TIP

High-volume e-mail accounts such as those available at www.gmail.com can be used to transfer an iTunes Library to another computer; use Winzip to zip groups of five folders together and e-mail them to yourself using gmail, and then retrieve them from the other computer.

one trick you absolutely need to know. Here's how (assuming you're already connected to the Internet).

Migrate Your Music Collection to a New Computer

1. If you have folders of music anywhere else but in the default location where iTunes puts them normally, you'll need to bring those folders to the new computer manually—or, if you have enough disc space, have iTunes copy all the music listed in the iTunes Library from wherever it is on your computer, to the default iTunes directory so you can grab everything in one chunk to put it on an external hard drive. To do this, go to **Advanced | Consolidate Library** and choose a location on the external hard drive to save your consolidated iTunes Library to.

   -or-

2. If you don't have a hard drive, burn data CDs or DVDs of all the music in your iTunes Library to bring to the new computer. Physically move your whole iTunes music folder (in Windows, it's in **My Documents\My Music\iTunes**) to the new computer using your weapon of choice: an external hard drive, an online storage locker, your home network, or burned data CDs or DVDs.

3. Put the iTunes Library in the default location—the same place it was on the computer you got it from (most likely **My Documents\My Music\iTunes**).

4. Install iTunes on the new machine.

5. Try to play a song you purchased from iTunes Music Store. iTunes will ask you for your username and password; fill those out (Figure 10-6), and that song and all the others you've purchased should be authorized for playback on the new computer.

Figure 10-6: No, I won't tell you my password.

Figure 10-7: Unlike other music services, Apple makes this menu item easy to find . . . classy.

TIP

You can sometimes find your iPod's music using Windows itself. Open up the iPod folder (with external hard drive use enabled) and go to **Tools** | **Folder Options** | **View** and select **Show Hidden Folders And Files**. If you see numbered folders, double-click them; your iPod's songs are inside those folders.

6. On the old computer, go to **Advanced I Deauthorize Computer** (Figure 10-7). (Skip this step if you want to leave the songs on the old computer!)

Power Up with Red Chair Anapod Explorer (Windows)

iTunes is great, and even the most advanced Jedi has to use it every now and again. But if you're ready for it, a whole new frontier of functionality is yours for the taking in a program designed by a solo developer: Red Chair Software's Anapod Explorer (www.redchairsoftware.com, free–$30, depending on whether you go with the trial version or not). The trial version has limited functionality but does include the ability to edit playlists and search. You can also browse your iPod's Library in Windows but can't move music on and off the iPod via Windows drag-and-drop. The full version can do that and much more.

Use Anapod Manager

Once you install Anapod Explorer, you'll see a little white iPod in your Windows taskbar. When your iPod's connected, right-click that icon for a pop-up box, offering easy access to Anapod Explorer, Xstreamer, and more.

Get Total Freedom, Have Complete Control

With Anapod Explorer installed, you can double-click the My Computer icon on your desktop and have your iPod show up. You might be thinking you can already do this without the program installed by enabling your iPod to be used as an external disc and clicking **iPod** in **My Computer**. The difference is that with Anapod, you'll see an icon for Anapod Explorer instead. Double-clicking it brings up a different, far more functional view (Figure 10-8) than what you get with Windows.

Anapod Explorer allows one-touch synchronization of your complete iTunes Library or certain folders.

Since Anapod Explorer gives you more control than iTunes does, you could potentially transfer music onto your iPod and delete it from your computer. When you want to listen to the iPod at your desk, you could connect it and play the songs back from the iPod over your computer's sound system. However, since you might (though we hope not) lose or damage your iPod when you're out and about, we don't recommend this as a general practice.

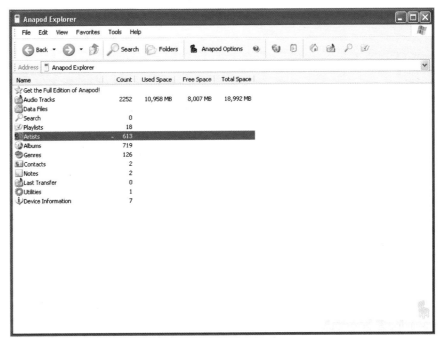

Figure 10-8: *You can drag and drop songs back and forth from your iPod to your computer, search, and more, by double-clicking any of these categories.*

Set up a password for your iPod so that Recording Industry Artists Association (RIAA) spider programs don't mistake you for a music pirate, necessitating the potential retention of a good lawyer on your part and a legal settlement to the RIAA (a legal consortium of labels), courtesy of your checking account.

Turn Your iPod into a Website

The potential for copyright infringement is fairly high with this feature that puts your iPod's Library on the Web with a full interface. Red calls it Anapod Xstreamer, and it lets anyone with your iPod's URL right-click and download any song on your iPod using a normal Web browser (although they won't be able to play anything you purchased from the iTunes Music Store). It's a great way for you to access your own iPod's music from another location, but it stands to reason that you wouldn't want to attract too much attention to that URL on message boards and the like.

ColorWare specializes in covering various electronics devices with a layer of resilient paint. Send your iPod to them and it'll come back much more unique than it was before you sent it in. We have experience with ColorWare's iPod coloring service and have found it to be reputable. However, they do not assume responsibility for data stored on your iPod, so make sure to back up everything on there to your computer's hard drive before you send your iPod off.

1. Browse www.colorwarepc.com for the color you want. You can pay extra for "color combinations," which most commonly paint the front of an iPod one color and the scroll wheel another. Arrows are usually painted white or black, whichever helps them stand out more.

2. You'll see prices listed underneath the various models. That's because ColorWare sells pre-painted iPods (and laptops and game consoles, for that matter) in various configurations and over 20 colors. If you'd rather buy a new iPod than have your old one painted, you can buy one on the site. Otherwise continue to step 3.

3. At the top of the ColorWare website, click **Services**, and on the next page, choose **Apple Services**.

4. Here, choose either **Apple iPod** (one color, more variety, $50–$65) or **Apple iPod Color Combos** (two colors, less variety, $85).

5. Choose your color, clicking **View Options** to see what each one looks like. Then, pick your iPod model (see Chapter 1 for help with that, if you're in doubt).

Continued . . .

Get Tunes Off the iPod

What happens if all the music that you've spent months (maybe years?) accumulating comes to a crashing end? Hard disk failures can happen anytime, and you should prepare for them by backing up your data. But backing up 40 GB of data can be hard to do; what if you've been lazy with it and are now fretting? Well, fret no more. There exist several programs that let you get music off of the iPod as well as on to it.

The iPod's hard disk works like any other, so freely managing your own data shouldn't require additional programs like this. However, Apple added functions that prevent copying music files from it. While this makes short-sighted sense as an effort to slow file sharing, it is pretty annoying to buy something that's purposefully crippled.

iPod Agent (www.ipodsoft.com) is one program that lets you move music and other files in both directions. It also adds some extra handy functions like loading local movie times to your iPod. We like that it also helps text users load text files bigger than the iPod limit of 4K by breaking them up into smaller files.

Podcast Your Own Music or Talk Show

Have you become hooked on podcasting? If so you might want to try your hand at it—it's getting easier, thanks to advances in audio recording software. You might even find dedicated podcasting software.

Acquire What You Need to Podcast

It takes surprisingly little gear to turn your vocal cord vibrations into a podcast for anyone in the world to tune into using iTunes or an iPod (other MP3 players also play podcasts).

GETTING A PAINT JOB

(*Continued*)

6. If you own an iPod dock, still use the earbuds that came with the iPod, or use an iTrip FM transmitter, consider getting that colored the same tone ($10–$20 each).

7. Pay for the service on colorwarepc.com, or use the alternate payment options (or call the customer service number).

8. Print out the order slip from ColorWare's website and fill it out.

9. Box your iPod up into the packaging it came with if you had it shipped; otherwise, put it in the original box and put that inside another cardboard box, perhaps with Styrofoam peanuts or other more environmentally friendly padding.

10. Attach the order slip you printed out in step 8 and send it off to the address specified on ColorWare's site (in Winona, Minnesota).

11. You'll get your iPod back in about 10 days, and we bet you'll be astounded by the new coating, which gets rid of old scratches and is more resistant to new ones.

HAVE SOMETHING TO SAY

Unless you're utterly hilarious, knowledgeable, and insightful when discussing any and all topics at length, try to pick a focus for your show. Whether it's world news, sports, gardening, fashion, music, technology, cars, bridal planning, bicycle touring, tree leaping, tea-steeping, beekeeping, or jet skiing . . . well, you get the picture. A focused show also helps you come up with a title and gives potential listeners a way to find your podcast needle in the podcast haystack.

GET A MICROPHONE

Assuming you'll be doing some speaking, you'll want a microphone and probably something to hold it up. (There are also screen attachments that keep your vowel sounds like "p" or "b" from exploding in listeners' ears.) Radio Shack and eBay are two places to look first for something cheap. You can also get decent results with the cheapo little microphones that come with many desktop computers, or maybe even a USB microphone used for gaming. Connect this mic to your computer's microphone input (usually a red-ringed jack near the headphone jack).

BUY PODCASTING SOFTWARE (OPTIONAL)

Rather than using a mishmash of various free programs to create your podcast, you could pay for something like MixMeister Propaganda (www.mixmeister .com), which handles everything: recording, editing, mixing down, encoding to MP3, adding the RSS/XML text wrapper, and uploading your new show to your server. You'll have to enter your show and server information the first time you use the program, but once you have that installed, it's smooth sailing. Other options include Winpodcast, iPodcast Creator, PodProducer, and more (search the Web for words such as podcast, or podcast software).

FIND A PODCAST HOST

Some online service providers now offer specialized podcast packages that are designed specifically for hosting podcasts. It pays to shop around; *podcasting* is

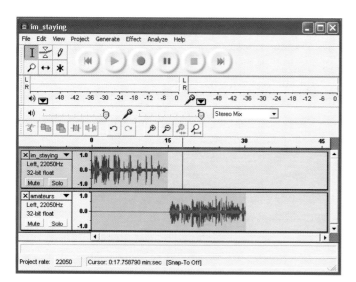

Figure 10-9: *Audacity's free to use, and surprisingly, more stable on Windows, Mac, and Linux than most proaudio editing suites.*

Figure 10-10: Once you have everything imported and lined up, all you have to do is export this show as an MP3 (File | Export As MP3), and Audacity will mix it down to a podcastable format.

such a buzzword that all sorts of profiteers are out there trying to snag some of the market, and you need to make sure you get a competitive rate.

GET AUDIO SOFTWARE

You'll need some audio recording and editing software like Audacity (Figure 10-9, audacity.sourceforge.net), Goldwave (goldwave.com), or Sound Forge. Audacity is free and has nice tutorials on how to use the program.

INCLUDE BACKGROUND MUSIC

Even if your podcast isn't about music, adding clips and sound effects can give your podcast extra zing. Some podcasting applications let you trigger sounds with certain keys on your keyboard so you can add them live, but you'll probably find that it's easier to add music and sound effects in what media pros call "post," which stands for "post-production." The audio editing software we recommend, Audacity, lets you add extra tracks with ease by clicking **Project | Import Audio** and navigating to the file you want to add (Figure 10-10).

USE A TEXT EDITOR

You can use a text editor to create the XML file that describes your program to the world. This must be a text-only file—word processor files such as DOC files won't do (although you can use Microsoft Word if you chose **File | Save As** and select TXT file (Plain Text) from the drop-down menu). Your Windows or Macintosh computer also came with a text editor built right into the operating system: WordPad in Windows (**Start | Programs | Accessories | WordPad**) or SimpleText on a Mac.

CREATING YOUR OWN PODCAST

Here's the basic idea, although we left this section a little bare intentionally. Podcasting is still such a new medium that there aren't many programs around to simplify the process of wrapping your MP3 in an RSS feed yet. A little online research should yield some decent freeware or shareware podcasting applications for download.

1. Record the show; we recommend that you use Audacity (audacity.sourceforge.net), which has everything you need and doesn't cost a dime. See Chapter 9 for more podcasting resources.

2. Edit the audio, removing any verbal missteps ("uh, um, err, you know what I mean," etc.). You can also run noise reduction and hiss reduction, but in general, a dry mix works fine for podcasting your voice.

3. Export it as an MP3; a bit rate of 64 Kbps should be sufficient. If your podcast is voice only, consider mixing it down to one mono track, since that takes up half the space and recordings made with most desktop microphones are mono anyway.

4. Make an XML file with all the relevant data about your recording.

5. Post the MP3s and XML file on your server, using whatever directions your host service provides.

6. Publicize your podcast by submitting it to podcast directories (a simple web search will turn up several, but you might start at iPodder.org, Podcast.net, or PodCastAlley.com).

7. Keep doing your show every week; who knows, you might be able to build up enough of a following to influence the *New York Times* Best Sellers list like Oprah, or you might end up being approached by a nationwide detergent company to advertise their wares during your dramatic daytime soap opera show.

MusicBrainz (Windows)

Like today's commercial Gracenote CD identification database (which identifies CDs in iTunes and other CD rippers), the MusicBrainz database was collaboratively developed by a community of users. Aim it at your MP3 collection and it'll fix all of those songs with missing song information. This is crucial, since iPod and iTunes both rely on this song information for listing info. You want your song data to be complete and uniform, and this program addresses both of those concerns.

1. Go to www.musicbrainz.org and sign up for an account by clicking the Login button at the top and selecting **Create A New Account.**

2. Download MusicBrainz Tagger for Windows from www.musicbrainz.org.

3. Click **File | Open Folder** (Figure 10-11) and select the folder your MP3s are stored in. Look at the status bar and wait until the program's done analyzing all of the tracks in that directory and all of its subdirectories.

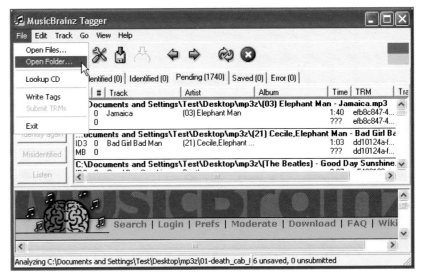

Figure 10-11: Pick a folder; MusicBrainz Tagger will go to work on every MP3 in that directory. This could take a while!

NOTE

MusicBrainz doesn't work on AAC files purchased from the iTunes Music Store, but that's okay because they're tagged properly anyway. However, it does work on unprotected AAC files you've ripped from your own CDs by importing them into iTunes.

CAUTION

We're not joking about MusicBrainz taking a long time to process large collections. You may even want to let it run overnight. The reason it takes so long is that it actually listens to each song and compares its acoustic fingerprint to an online database—complicated, but it can all take place while you're sleeping.

CAUTION

Before MusicBrainz can work, you'll need an account there (just as with Audioscrobbler, covered next). Click the **Login** link at the bottom of the MusicBrainz main page, and then click **Create New Login** and follow the directions. You can do this either before or after starting the MusicBrainz program (**Start | Programs | MusicBrainz**).

4. You can also track the progress by looking at numbers in the **Unidentified, Identified,** and **Pending** tabs. When they stop changing, MusicBrainz Tagger is done analyzing and correcting your library.

5. While MusicBrainz Tagger runs through your MP3 library (or, if it's small, after it's done), click the various tabs or resort the lists by clicking the column headers (**Track, Artist, Time, Album,** etc.).

6. Click MusicBrainz Tagger's **Unidentified** tab. That's where MusicBrainz puts the songs it isn't sure about. These songs require a little human intervention on your part to add information to them. To do that, select a song and click **Listen.** Click **Lookup** to bring up the screen on which you can identify the song.

7. Expand the MusicBrainz Tagger window so that it takes up the entire screen so you can see the bottom pane, where you can modify the information for the selected song. This part's self-explanatory; just keep in mind that you'll need to provide real song information and verify your e-mail address. The information you submit will go to other users as well, and you wouldn't want to pollute the system.

8. Proofread the program's guesses in the **Identified** tab by matching your song info with the MusicBrainz database's suggestion, selecting songs and clicking **Listen** to bring up your default MP3 playback software. If the suggestion is wrong, click **Misidentified;** if it's right, keep scrolling down the list.

9. When you're satisfied with MusicBrainz' accuracy, click the **Write ID3 Tags To Files** button (Figure 10-12). You'll see the number in the **Identified** tab decrease and the number in the **Saved** tab increase, reflecting the re-tagging of your MP3 and AAC files.

Figure 10-12: Clicking this button tells MusicBrainz Tagger to add missing information to all of the music files listed under the Identified tab.

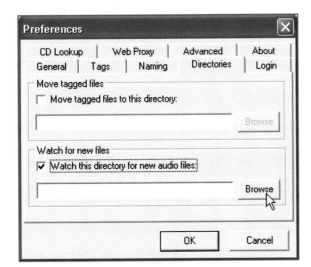

Figure 10-13: *This window lets you tweak settings to optimize the program, but other than the Login and Directories tabs, you don't need to mess with much else.*

10. Click the **View/Change Options** button to bring up the **Preferences** window (Figure 10-13); browse through the tabs; everything's fairly self-explanatory. The **Directories** tab holds one highlight: the ability to watch a specific directory for new files. If you choose the folder you usually rip and download MP3s to, MusicBrainz will analyze new MP3s every time you run it.

11. Before you exit the Preferences window, go to the **Login** tab (Figure 10-14) and enter the username and password you chose on www.musicbrainz.com back in step 1.

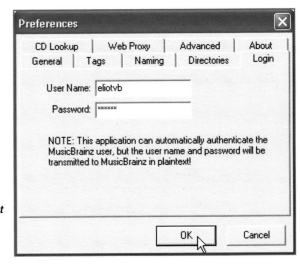

Figure 10-14: *Enter your account info here and you're all set.*

Jay Tuley's iEatBrainz (for Mac)

The Mac version of MusicBrainz is called iEatBrainz. It's also free and open-source; the work of a computer science student. It may or may not work with your specific combination of Mac OS X and iTunes. That said, when it works, it's just as effective as the Windows-only MusicBrainz application. iEatBrainz works on MP3s and AACs, and you can find it at www.indyjt.com (or by searching the Web for *iEatBrainz*).

RAISING THE TOP VOLUME OF A EUROPEAN iPOD

Apple's iPod is one of the more powerful portable audio devices sold in America, with a 30 mW-per-channel output that can drive most headphones just fine. However, some iPods sold in Europe have volumes that were lowered by mandate of the European Union because of a French law designed to prevent hearing loss in the general population due to excessive volume in such devices. You can pump up the volume on one of these iPods using one of the following downloadable programs:

- **euPod's VolumeBoost (www.eupod.com, Windows only)** This one's free to use, although the developer does request a beer donation. That said, it now has several impressive features aside from VolumeBoost, including MP3Gain, numbered battery display, encryption to protect your iPod's data, and more.

- **iPodVolumeBooster (volumebooster .tangerine-soft.de, Mac only)** This program is focused only on raising the volume limit of European iPods, but it's also free.

The Audioscrobbler Plug-In (Mac and Windows)

This plug-in runs inside of iTunes, checking out what you're playing and sending the data to the audioscrobbler.com online database. This might sound a bit nefarious, but take comfort in the fact that Audioscrobbler (Figure 10-15) is a not-for-profit open-source initiative that only uses the data to run a song

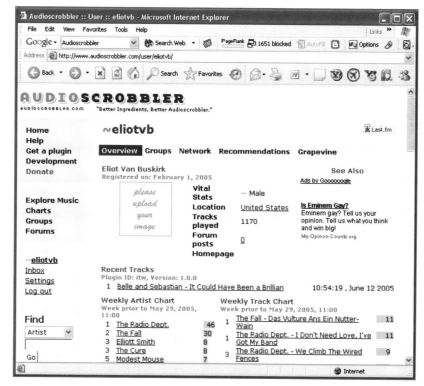

Figure 10-15: Audioscrobbler is only a plug-in that sits inside of iTunes, relatively invisibly. The program's interface is on audioscrobbler.com, once you sign in.

If you're deep into blogging, check out another plug-in called WMPTuneLog (www.minimalverbosity.com). As the name suggests, it works with Windows Media Player, but it works equally well with iTunes. It's a bit complicated, requiring you to insert different bits of code into your feeds depending on which blogging service you use; check out the F.A.Q. area of the site for more information.

recommendation engine and give you information back about what you're playing from multiple locations, unlike iTunes' own play tracking mechanism.

1. First, you need to sign up for an Audioscrobbler account at www.audioscrobbler.com by clicking the link on the left side that says **Sign Up Now.**

2. Then, click the **Get A Plugin** link on the left and download and install the plug-in for either Windows or Mac, depending on which you're using.

3. Continue using iTunes as you normally would. To check your Audioscrobbler profile, click your name when signed into the site. You'll be able to see which bands and songs you've been listening to the most in the past week and since you've had the plug-in installed.

4. Explore the rest of the site for forums, groups, your network, artist recommendations, or any friends you might have that also use Audioscrobbler.

A

How To...

- *Got Convenience If You Want It*
- *Low-Range FM Radio Broadcasting*
- *Mock Cassette Tape*
- *Direct Input*
- *Get a New Receiver*
- *Hook Up Your Shuffle*
- *But I Don't Want To Share— I Just Want Power!*

Appendix
Putting Wheels on Your iPod (or an iPod in Your Wheels)

For many, the car is where the most concentrated music listening takes place. No matter what set of wheels you drive, short daily commutes and long road trips greatly benefit from an iPod full of music pumping from the speakers inside those wheels.

This appendix will help you integrate your iPod into your car in the right way for you. In other words, we'll go over the most popular methods of achieving automotive poditude.

Why Put an iPod in My Car?

Maybe you're happy with the radio, or you can't live without your collection of moldy mix tapes from past romantic interests. Or maybe you're just afraid that an installation will be more trouble than it's worth. There are solutions to all of these worries, and as usual, the only thing limiting your ability to rock the iPod in your car is your willingness to spend just a little more money. And dude! You know it's worth it; otherwise you wouldn't have spent the money on the iPod in the first place.

The obvious general advantage to having an iPod hooked into your car stereo is that you're able to play all of your iPod's music wherever you drive, without the dangerous option of resorting to headphones. Other passengers can listen too, and won't accuse you of being antisocial. And because of the vast resource of your iPod's library, you'll always have the right song for any mood that strikes. No more being stuck with just your Metallica CDs on a hot date that calls for a different mood.

Got Convenience If You Want It

As far as using the iPod as your main source of car audio, there are some differences in terms of convenience. When in use, even the most sophisticated installations call for your full attention when the time comes to make any programming changes. Never assume that you can juggle any iPod tasks while you drive. The same, however, goes with changing a CD. (One of us has a very good friend who must now use a wheelchair after his girlfriend lost control of the car while changing the disc—this really is serious business. Don't forget.)

Having a playlist is a key advantage that frees your hands and sets your mind at ease. Most CDs end at 70 minutes maximum, while you could conceivably program a playlist that would get you from San Diego, California, to Portland, Maine, and back, without ever changing a thing.

Types of Car Installations

First, you need to decide which type of iPod installation fits both your car's current system and your own budget. Listed next are the major connection types to choose from.

Before proceeding, it's worth checking if your carmaker has an iPod kit. Or more specifically, it's worth checking on this if your mechanics tend to be European types. The latest range of Euro-chic machines all seem to have iPod options. Neither American nor Japanese carmakers, however, aside from Nissan, have been as quick to jump on this trend. Too bad.

Low-Range FM Radio Broadcasting

This is the most basic of the methods used, and with no wires involved it's the cleanest and probably the best way to get you started. All you need is to buy an add-on to your iPod that will take its signal and broadcast it to a channel that your car radio can receive.

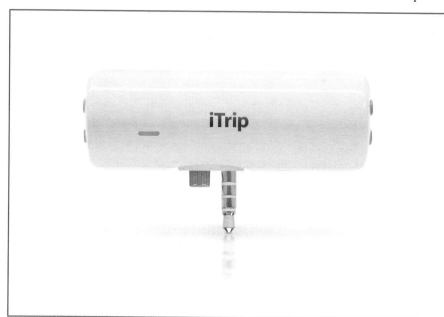

- **Benefits**   Low cost, easy installation. There are no wires to hook up, no extra hardware (aside from the unit, which usually fits right on the iPod).

- **Advantages**   Fairly cheap; most products that use this system are easily portable.

- **Disadvantages**   When this type of unit first came out, reception was mixed (pun intended). In locations with a lot of free spaces on the radio dial, you could count on tuning in pretty easily. But in urban centers where the radio spectrum is as tight as the housing markets, it was sometimes impossible to operate without interference.

The iTrip by Griffin is the standard and has a remarkably clean add-on (Figure A-1) that fits the iPod look (there's even a black and red U2 model). The RoadTrip (also by Griffin) and the XtremeMac AirPlay have stepped up with some better features.

*Figure A-1: **The iTrip by Griffin set the pace for the FM radio iPod transmitters but has recently been superceded by a few upstarts.***

Mock Cassette Tape

This is for those who love the look and feel of cassette tapes but want the advantage of wires coming out of them. Seriously, a faux cassette tape that serves as an input for iPod signals is kind of an ingenious hack, and if you're still driving a car that came with a cassette player (count one of us in this category), it's a cheap and easy add-on. iTrip-maker Griffin has just released a new, improved iPod cassette interface called the SmartDeck that accepts some feedback from the cassette player, offering limited control over some vital iPod functions (Figure A-2).

- **Advantages** Easy to use, retro-geek-cool, cheap, no installation.
- **Disadvantages** Sound quality is not as good as direct input.

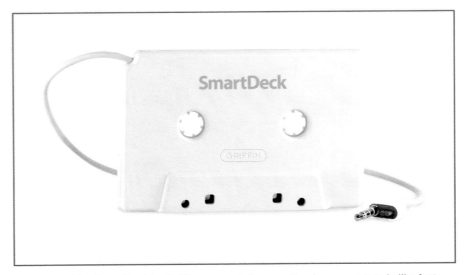

Figure A-2: ***The SmartDeck by Griffin responds to cassette player commands like fast forward for next song, reverse to skip back.***

Direct Input

If your car's player allows direct input from external devices, there's no question that this method is the way to go: it offers much better sound quality than cassette or FM transmitters. Most receivers, aside from those that come factory-installed with your car, have this capability.

A very elegant solution, if your car stereo is supported, is the ice>Link Plus by Dension, which really does it all: it hooks directly in and charges your iPod while providing a sturdy place to keep it. You can even control the iPod from your receiver. Luxurious and good looking, it is, not surprisingly, on the expensive side. See www.dension.com/icelink_info.htm.

Get a New Receiver

If you've got the money to install a whole new receiver for your car, you should take a look at new systems by car stereo stalwart Alpine that recently added very impressive iPod playback and even charging capabilities.

Hook Up Your Shuffle

Shuffle owners need not feel left out when it comes to moving and grooving. The DLO Transpod for iPod Shuffle is just the thing to hook up your tiny iPod to your car stereo in high style, using the standard FM transmitter technology popular with bigger units.

The cool thing about this Transpod is that it picks up its style right where the Shuffle leaves off (Figure A-3), and it doesn't look as derivative as many other iPod accessories. Without the wannabe iPod design, you're left with a pretty cool device that fits your car without making it look like it got a Macintosh makeover.

Figure A-3: *The DLO Transpod for iPod Shuffle lets you hook up the littlest iPod with ease and style.*

Mount Your iPod

Not like a horse, of course. You'll want someplace secure and handy to keep your iPod in your car. Some systems, particularly the pricey ones, come with their own mounting systems. For others, you'll need to shop around.

Since chances are you've already got a cup holder, there are several popular mounts that take advantage of this sturdy real estate to firmly grip your Pod. TuneDok Car Holder from Belkin (maker of the iTrip), the PodPod by Griffin, and the Cup Holder Car Mount by Everything iPod are holders below $35 that have been around a while.

But I Don't Want To Share—I Just Want Power!

Say you don't need to blast your tunes from your car's speakers. Maybe you're a (nondriving) teenager who likes to use those headphones to avoid listening to your family during the long hours of vacation, but you want to make sure your iPod has enough juice to last. Unlike what your parents might have implied, you, my friend, are actually very easy to satisfy. There are now many types of adapters that draw power from car lighters.

Belkin's iPod Car Charger is a good, cheap solution at $19.95. There are many others like it.

The Future

Several models of car come with wireless Bluetooth connections that enable drivers to talk on the phone over the car's speaker system (generally using the mounted cell phone's mic for the speaking part). Considering the recent availability of wireless headphones for the iPod that use a similar type of wireless Bluetooth connection, it's likely that you'll eventually be able to beam music into your car stereo without wires, in perfect digital quality.